W9-AYE-803

PERPETUAL
MOTIVATION

PERPETUAL MOTIVATION

How to Light Your Fire and
Keep It Burning in Your Career and in Life

DAVE DURAND

*Pro*Balance INC

_Pro_Balance ɪɴᴄ

▲

P.O.Box 298
Big Bend, WI 53103-0298
U.S.A.

ISBN 0-9675631-0-0
Self help / Business

To those readers committed to change.

Acknowledgements

This book was made possible over the years through the efforts of many friends and acquaintances. The study of what really motivates people can't be effective without the cooperation of literally thousands of individuals.

I thank all the wonderful people I've had the opportunity to work with over the past ten years while compiling this treatise. Nearly everyone I've interacted with in some small way helped shape the formula for motivation discussed in these pages.

In order to effectively determine what really motivates a person, one must spend a vast amount of time both in triumph and tribulation with many different people. To those willing to share their experiences, I am deeply grateful.

I thank my wife, Lisa, for her incredible support of this project. One secret not revealed in this book is how to marry someone as wonderful as she is. I believe God gave us to each other, and I thank Him for her role in my life which, because of her, is filled with motivation.

I also thank—

My children, Kevin, Nicole, Ethan and our new arrival, Hannah. You are filled with love and remind me daily of the importance and the rewards of balance in life.

My parents, Tom and Marty, for their living example and wonderful upbringing.

My siblings, Pete, Dan, Kathy, and Mary, for their unique roles in shaping my thoughts.

Don Freda, who's example as a leader helped shape me in the first years of my business career.

Marty Domitrovich, who helped teach me the art of focus.

Erick Laine, Mike Lancellot, and all the executives at Vector.

Warren Jamison, for his professionalism and editorial assistance.

Contents

"Motivation will almost always beat mere talent."

—— Norman A. Augustine

Introduction

No matter where your level of motivation stands today, you will be able to benefit by a renewed ability to be motivated beyond your greatest expectations. You will find that *you can do it!*

When you begin reading a book about motivation it makes sense to ask,

"Am I motivated enough to become *more* motivated?"

It's a fair question. Many people wrongly associate motivation directly with effort. They think—or feel—something like this: "To *be* five times more motivated, I'd have to *try* five times harder than I do now."

When unmotivated people look at someone who is highly motivated, they are often quick to give up—thinking they just don't have what it takes to live a highly motivated life. In the pits of de-motivation, thousands of mentally capable and physically healthy born-and-raised Americans are homeless drifters in their own country.

Compare them to Hiroaki Aoki, who arrived in the U.S. before he could make himself understood in English. This tremendous disadvantage has de-motivated millions of immigrants before him. After adopting a name Americans could pronounce easily, Rocky Aoki set about making his dreams come true. Motivated to work seven days a week selling ice cream in New York City, he slept in storerooms to save money. Through saving and borrowing, Rocky scraped together enough money to finance his first four-table restaurant in New York. Now his international Benihana chain has served over 100 million meals and he is wealthy far beyond the dreams of the struggling young immigrant. Sure, Rocky had a unique concept in food service, certainly he had great timing, but it would have amounted to nothing if he had lacked motivation.

Motivation is related to effort but more importantly, it's related to strategy, focus, and timing. It's like lifting with a lever instead of with brute strength. The lever is what makes lifting easier just as strategy and focus make living a motivated life easier. Some people exert enough energy in life to get big results but they don't use a lever to multiply their efforts. Highly motivated people are able to focus on the areas of life that will fuel additional motivation and give their efforts tremendous leverage.

Being motivated brings a priceless sense of unparalleled completeness and happiness. The question is, how do we achieve this priceless level of motivation? We all know highly motivated people. We also know highly unmotivated people. What makes these people so different? Which one are you? Or are you somewhere in the middle?

Some people just seem to have the inner drive to handle all of life's responsibilities and to achieve success. What drives them? What motivates them? Are they different from you and me in some fundamental way? To the last question I can give a quick answer: no, they aren't different in some basic way.

For the past decade, I've studied what motivates people. My ten-year scrutiny involved working with thousands of businesspeople, a host of athletes, many parents and many children. Add to that list, extensive self-examination.

As each year passed, I felt closer to answering the question: "What motivates people?" As my knowledge grew, I learned to help more people tap into their own ability to motivate themselves. By developing and focusing on key components, we can all learn to be the type of person who has the inner drive to get the most out of life.

Now, finally, ten years after I began my research, I am confident that the following Formula for Motivation will help motivate you toward success. This formula can act as your lever to enormously enhance your life through the power of motivation.

Motivation *equals*

The Pursuit of Life's Perfect Balance

plus **Influence**

plus **Creativity**

plus **Sense of Humor**

minus **Runaway Self-Esteem**

or

Motivation = B + I + (C + H) − RSE

With its several components, the Formula for Motivation is far more powerful than the popular two-word admonition, *be positive*. As does much of the material published today on the subject of motivation, *be positive* greatly oversimplifies the solution of the basic problem: How do I motivate myself to begin with; and, once motivated, how can I be sure I will stay motivated for the rest of my life?

It would be nice if the Formula for Motivation had fewer components, but it does not. Each component is vital and each relies on the other parts. The fuel allowing a person to stay motivated and remain effective is the combination of all the components working together like a well-oiled machine. As with any machine, if one part isn't working the whole machine can't function properly, or even work at all. Likewise, if a person possesses all the components for motivation except one, say creativity, the person won't be as effective and his motivation to put forth continued effort will be weak.

It's easy to fall into the trap of saying, "I have everything the formula includes. I'm funny, a good communicator, well balanced, humble and very creative." These things may all be true. My question to you is, how do these traits fit together in your life?

Even if you are a motivated person by virtue of possessing those traits, you can take your motivation to a higher level. Just having these traits alone does not constitute a motivated person in the same way that owning land, lumber, bricks and mortar doesn't make you a homeowner. Only by applying intelligence and skilled labor to assemble these elements will you have a home.

Being motivated in life doesn't happen automatically, often we need to put forth a great deal of effort to enjoy the fruits of our labor. Achieving this fulfillment and satisfaction are really what motivates us during our daily activities.

Throughout the book I will explain in greater detail what is involved in each of the components of the formula for motivation. You will come to understand how motivation is achieved and maintained by incorporating these concepts into your daily lifestyle.

At first you may think the formula for motivation may not come naturally, but the more you weave it into your way of life, the more you will realize how natural it really is.

During my many years of training people and researching success principles, I came across a select group of people who excelled through outstanding motivation. These motivated people usually left a great impression on others. People remember a motivated individual long after an event, an accomplishment, even a lifetime. I call people who achieve the highest level of motivation *Legacy Achievers*.

I am not a scientist, neither am I psychologist. Because of this, my research is based primarily on observation and personal experience, not on scientific studies. The observations I've made involved literally thousands of people and took more than ten years to crystallize in my mind into a fully developed and teachable action philosophy.

Throughout the book I portray legacy achievers as though they all think, talk, behave, and believe the exact same things to simplify the material. Obviously everyone is a little—or a lot—different in their philosophies and actions. Nevertheless, in basic things, legacy achievers, as a group, have much in common and run true to form. In many different ways they all embody the effectiveness of the Formula for Motivation given here. They are the ideal examples of highly motivated and well-balanced people.

Legacy achievers are able to achieve success in their careers as well as in all aspects of their lives. They balance the priorities and responsibilities of family, finances, health, social contributions, faith and their careers. When these are in balance, success follows and happiness abounds.

To become a legacy achiever, you must work through other phases of life along the way. Inspired by a philosophy of Mike Lancellot's, the CEO of Vector Marketing, I call the first phase the *Making a Name* Phase. I call the second phase the *Building a Reputation* Phase.

To illustrate the process of becoming a legacy achiever, I will present a work-related example. Keep in mind that becoming a legacy achiever is not only about becoming successful at work. Use this example to parallel other areas of your life.

Very often, when people start new jobs, they don't even make it to the first phase, Making a Name. For others, making a name in a job may occur in a few weeks or a few years, depending on the industry.

A person makes a name for himself or herself when supervisors or peers become aware of great performance. In automobile sales, this awareness may occur in a matter of weeks. Most likely, the managers and other salespeople feel great about working with a successful, motivated new person and see a bright future for her or him.

In other industries such as pharmaceutical sales, engineering, or computer software development, it may take as long as several years to make a name. Likewise, it often takes self-employed people a greater period of time to reach this level of recognition in their industry or community.

Some people never make it past this phase. They may feel motivated for a short time and experience some success. But then they drift away, often because neglected problems in their lives reach a crescendo of chaos, and the pieces fall apart. With no balance in their lives, motivation vanishes.

Others sustain the *making a name* phase long enough to reach the next one, which is *Building a Reputation*. In this second phase, motivated people become independent at work and are relied on by co-workers because they produce positive and predictable results.

People who appear to be successfully building a reputation generally use three or more of the Motivation Formula's components, but they don't use all five of them. Thus, their reputation building stage lasts only for a short time until they reach a point in their lives when they say, "I can't go on like this anymore." It means burnout has struck again. Suddenly the afflicted person quits, leaving everybody at work wondering why.

We're often caught off guard by such an event because on the outside they seemed to have everything together. Like a car washed and waxed regularly, we can't see any flaws. But problems under the hood can stop the most beautifully polished car from moving forward.

All of us lack motivation and balance at some point in our lives. For some of us, regaining motivation simply takes an oil change at life's motivational quick-lube. Others, need a complete engine overhaul.

If we are not in balance in one or more aspects of life, we feel uneasy and this anxiety contaminates the other areas. This makes it difficult to concentrate on the task at hand. We are more effective if we are attending to all of our responsibilities in a balanced fashion.

People who advance to the reputation-building level can then become legacy achievers by using all components of the Formula for Motivation. When legacy achievers leave a job—always by choice, not necessity—they leave behind a record of accomplishment that is long remembered.

Think of the challenge faced by the person who takes over the role of a legacy achiever after the achiever retires or goes on to greater challenges and opportunities. Can you imagine the pressure felt by Phil Bengtson, the Green Bay Packers' new coach, after Vince Lombardi left the team?

Legacy achievers have a powerful impact at home, where their legacy and positive influence can live on through generations. Think of legacy achievers as people whose grandchildren and great grandchildren will speak of them endearingly and with admiration.

Legacy achievers are able to balance many priorities in life with what looks like very little effort. Legacy achievers find time to take good care of their health. They also handle finances for the long term while simultaneously enjoying life today. Legacy achievers become mainstays in the community and remain loyal to their faiths.

There are many well-known legacy achievers in the world such as best selling author Stephen Covey or the late Mother Theresa. But who are the legacy achievers in your life?

My parents, my grandmother, my first-grade teacher, one of my insurance agents, several business-people I work with, and many others come to mind as the legacy achievers in my life. These people's lives have impacted others not because they are famous but because they have an uncommon peace about them. Their examples are compelling even when their lessons contain no words. Legacy achievers build reputations, generate motivation, and enjoy the experience of success. Imagine such a life—fulfillment beyond your wildest dreams.

Consider this: being motivated is easy but staying motivated is not. It's something completely different. Think about it. How often have you said to yourself with great conviction, "My goal is to lose weight and I'm starting right now."

Or, "I'm going to be the number one salesperson."

Or, "I'm going to be the best manager."

Or, "I'm going to be the best parent in the world."

You're truly motivated for the moment. It may last only a few seconds. But for those few seconds, you are highly motivated.

Through my research, I wanted to learn what happens between those inspired seconds and the next moment when you find yourself uninspired, de-motivated, and actually negative about losing weight, being a great salesperson, or a better parent.

I learned the answer to sustaining the initial big bang of motivation isn't the sexy pat phrases we usually look for such as, "Think Big," or "You've got to believe to achieve." I found a much more practical answer in the Formula for Motivation, an answer that always works in spite of all discouragement.

Since each component in the formula is crucial, we need to focus on each one to develop the motivation that leads to success. Often with math formulas, it's necessary to begin at the end of the equation; likewise with the Formula for Motivation we begin with runaway self-esteem, the last component in the formula.

~ ~ ~

Part One

Ego and Balance

*Humility is not the renunciation of pride but
the substitution of one pride for another.*

—— Eric Hoffer

Chapter 1

The Killer—Runaway Self-esteem

If we use a mirror for our windshield, sooner or later we will crash. Boost your ability to motivate yourself by focusing on others. Perpetual motivation requires us to purge ourselves of the need to build self-esteem.

These statements contradict what most of us have been taught. At face value, self-esteem—meaning a *positive self-image*—is good. Here's the problem: while much material on how to build self-esteem is effective for living a fulfilling and motivated life, it's contaminated by half-truths and destructive advice finely woven through the effective ideas. This makes the harmful material hard to detect. Reading this chapter will help you identify the common dangers found in self-esteem materials that destroy our motivation.

Unfortunately, today's concept of self-esteem often leads to self-worship. This is because we are inundated with the importance of having a high self-esteem. Self-esteem has

> If we use a mirror for our windshield, sooner or later we will crash.

If we cross over the very fine line of healthy self-esteem, we enter into selfishness and become self-centered.

become an overvalued solution to our problems. Book after book tells us that a high self-esteem *produces* positive results and behavior in life. This is like spending money you don't have in the hope that you will earn it. In reality, healthy self-esteem is the *result* of positive behaviors, accomplishments and/or honoring predefined standards.

Whenever we focus on building self-esteem as the solution to our problems, we put the cart before the horse. This approach is ineffective and destructive. Focusing on building our self-esteem causes what I call runaway self-esteem.

If we cross over the very fine line of healthy self-esteem, we enter into selfishness and become self-centered.

Legacy achievers, however, receive so much fulfillment from focusing on important things in life outside their own skins that their results leave no need to focus on themselves.

To illustrate how runaway self-esteem takes a negative toll on every aspect of life and destroys motivation, I will present each balance point briefly here. Let's compare a person who has no need to build self-esteem to a person focused on self-esteem.

Runaway self-esteem in our:

Family ~

When a legacy achiever wakes up in the middle of the night to the sound of the baby crying, he focuses on the baby and his wife but not on himself. If he were to focus on himself,

he would conclude, "Getting up myself would not be fair. I have to go to work in the morning and I got up the last time."

Instead, he thinks about how much his wife, who never gets a spare moment during the day, could use the sleep. He thinks about how the baby is uncomfortable and needs to be changed. When the focus is not on ourselves the act of helping is easier.

Career ~

When legacy achievers are at work they think about helping the company perform better by doing their jobs to the best of their abilities. When in a leadership role, they focus on developing the people they lead to be the best they can be.

Legacy achievers feel a sense of accomplishment by watching the growth of each of their subordinates. As a result, their divisions grow and they will probably receive a pay raise or promotion without even asking for it.

If they were focused on themselves, they would think about how much overtime they worked, only to have their extra efforts go unrecognized. They would feel that Karen in the office across the hall gets more recognition, and more perks, than they do, even though her numbers are about the same.

They would think about how they could make more money at XYZ company, where they would be appreciated. As a result they go from job to job. They are equally unhappy everywhere; their temporary stays provide no opportunities for advancement; and their resumes soon reveal a pattern of job hopping that eliminates them from consideration by many companies.

Finances ~

When legacy achievers handle money, they think about what a privilege it is to have the money in the first place. They think about the responsibilities that come with it and invest it wisely for the future. They also contribute to charities. If they were to focus on themselves they would spend the money excessively on items that would enhance their self-image, or they would hoard it as a way to measure self-worth.

Faith ~

When legacy achievers focus on faith, they are governed not by their own opinions and pleasures but by God's laws. When they are faced with an ethical or moral decision, they ask themselves if the outcome of their actions would be offensive or pleasing to God. If they were focused on themselves they would choose whatever suits them best, as long as they could get away with it.

Health ~

When legacy achievers face health issues and concerns, they choose to eat properly and exercise because their health plays a powerful role in the lives of people around them. They respect their bodies as being gifts from God put in their care. Unfortunately, some people take better care of a VCR received as a gift than they do of their own bodies. Others, focused on self, go overboard and worship their bodies with excessive care in search of a more positive self-image.

Social Contributions ~

Legacy achievers focus on how past role models helped shape them throughout the years. As a result they contribute to social causes from which they may not receive a direct earthly reward. If they were focused on themselves they would never donate time, money, or talent without considering what they would get in return.

The greatest problem with self-esteem is the *self* part.

In a conversation with Dr. Ray Guarendi, a well-known lecturer and psychologist, I was intrigued when he said that self-esteem was a late twentieth century concoction. I was already researching self-esteem, although I hadn't taken a close look at its roots. Sure enough, authors did not focus on self-esteem before the middle of the twentieth century in the way many authors do today. For the most part, the early authors presented self-esteem as a result of behavior. Later authors present self-esteem as a means to behavior.

The notion that we need to run around engulfed in self-love would have appalled most people as recently as fifty years ago. Today magazines glorifying *self* fly off magazine racks; people buy products with "because I'm worth it!" tag lines. Our society has become wrapped up in the delusion of *self*.

Consider the popular self-esteem-building exercise: Look in the mirror every day and say twenty times, "I like myself. I like myself," and all your problems will disappear. Don't count on it.

In reality, you may have good reason for not liking yourself. Therefore, you may not buy into building your self-esteem by lying to yourself.

To suggest that you like yourself prior to changing the behavior that has been preventing you from liking yourself is foolish and simply doesn't work.

To suggest that you like yourself prior to changing the behavior that has been preventing you from liking yourself is foolish and simply doesn't work.

Yet, too often, this easy-way-out solution describes pop-culture today. Prior to the recent flood of self-love, people found esteem in other aspects of life. People measured self-worth through family, relationship with God, and a moral lifestyle.

The outside standard of natural law

Today, many people set self-esteem standards independently based on pop-culture influence—without the counsel of moral society.

The race for self-esteem starts at home. Overpraising children has become part of the culture of self-esteem. Many therapists and counselors are beginning to recognize the dangers in this. The November 22nd (1999) edition of the London Free Press quotes Cheryl Noble-MacGregor, a child and family therapist for the Institute for Family Living as saying, "Excessive praise becomes empty praise. It seems we are worshipping the god of self-esteem these days."

Many parents sell self-love to their children by suggesting, "Love yourself just because you're you." This circular logic demands no accountability.

It means that children do not need to act, talk, or behave to any set standard in order to feel good about who they are. When children are young they need to be given some outside perspective in order to ground their reason for their self-worth.

An example of an outside standard could be something as simple—yet as important—as being taught they are children of God. This can provide a solid footing, allowing the child to obey the natural law of right and wrong. This allows them to recognize their value even when their behavior doesn't reflect it.

Ignoring outside standards and natural law is advice readily found on the bookshelf. Typical of this advice is best-selling author Nathaniel Branden's book How to Raise Your Self-esteem. Dr Branden writes in his summary on page 153:

> Today, many people set self-esteem standards independently based on pop-culture influence—without the counsel of moral society.

"If we are to protect our self-esteem, we need to know how to assess appropriately our own behavior. This includes, *first, being certain that the standards by which we judge are truly our own, and not merely values of others to which we feel obligated to pay lip service.*" (Emphasis added.)

At face value this may sound like advice I might even give my children in circumstances where other kids might want to try drugs in order to be cool. I might say "don't pay attention to what those kids are saying; do what you know is right." The difference between what I would mean and Branden would mean is uncovered when you get a better understanding of his definition of *others*, which is "country, family, state, the true faith, society and more."

The reason I might tell my child to do what he "knows is right" is because he learned what is right and what is wrong from his mom and dad. Since Branden's followers are taught to disregard family and societal standards, the child would just have to determine if taking the drug would hurt or help his perceptions of self.

That statement summarizes an entire Branden chapter which teaches disregard of what most people call unselfish standards. This not only is an ineffective solution to a problem, it's also destructive.

When a child is not given a benchmark for earning self-respect, and instead sets his own self-esteem standards, the effects can be harmful. It is similar to a child making up all the rules at home in place of his parents. If this were the case he would proclaim: "I get candy any time I want and I get to go to bed as late as I want."

Independent standards would shove established standards aside and the child would be unaware of how damaging this would become. It takes a responsible, level-headed and mature person to establish rules of law and appropriate standards.

If employees practiced this philosophy they would disregard the leadership's standards for performance. Instead of feeling good about accomplishing what the company considers their standard of performance, Branden's disciples would make up their own. Anyone who has ever held a leadership position will tell you the employee-set standard will more than likely be lower and much less effective.

This thinking has already infiltrated the educational system. In some schools students grade themselves!

Too many people in society already live by this independent standard philosophy and as a result fail to pay

taxes, steal from their neighbors, and kill people. All because it fits into their standard.

In fairness to Dr. Branden, he does provide some very sound advice. It's advice I would give others and have learned from myself. In fact a thorough reading of his books shows that Dr. Branden believes, "We cannot work on self-esteem directly, neither our own nor anyone else's, because self-esteem is a *consequence*—such as that of living consciously, responsibly, purposefully, and with integrity. If we understand what those practices are we can commit to *initiating* them within ourselves and to dealing with others in such a way as to *facilitate* or *encourage* them to do likewise."(p.43 The Power of Self Esteem) I agree with this statement. But the theme of independent standards found elsewhere in his materials can be disturbing and destructive because it contradicts this sound advice.

Dr. Branden talks about the importance of responsibility, living purposefully, having morals and integrity, and even parents setting boundaries for their children. My question is, how does a person arrive at what is responsible, moral, or purposeful, if they are told to disregard others (as defined earlier) when it comes to their own standards for self-esteem? Dr Branden cannibalizes his own advice for his readers by providing these two very opposite perspectives.

Dr. Catherine Cardinal further demonstrates this in her book The Ten Commandments of Self-Esteem (Andrews McMeel Publishing). The first commandment she lists is "Thou shalt not consort with people that make thee feel bad about thyself." (Pg.5) Dr. Cardinal explains that if we associate with people that make us feel bad about ourselves we should leave the relationship, even if we have been in the relationship for some time.

If we play basketball without baskets, hockey without goals, and baseball without diamonds we would endlessly bicker about who won-scored-lost, yet no one would ever really know.

There is no mention in the chapter that a person may have a good reason to feel bad about themselves when they are in the company of certain people. Suppose a business partner of mine showed up to an important meeting unprepared. He should feel bad because that is the appropriate response to acting irresponsibly. Feeling bad is often what triggers us to improve.

To follow Dr. Cardinal's advice would, however, be to quit the job and go where others are also unprepared, so that you don't have to feel bad about your own behavior. I don't really believe Dr. Cardinal or Dr. Branden would tell someone to quit their job, but some people interpret self-esteem material as an all-encompassing self-preservation technique.

This is the problem, too much of this material lets us off the hook without having to change the behavior that makes us feel bad in the first place. What ever happened to the good old saying, "You should be ashamed of yourself?"

When you take away outside standards you take away the target. If we set our own standards without considering preset family, social, church, and company standards to name a few, we risk walking aimlessly through life, stripped of a significant source of our motivation. If we play basketball without baskets, hockey without goals, and baseball without diamonds we would endlessly bicker about who won-scored-lost, yet no one would ever really know.

Setting our standards without considering outside standards is like people saying, "I want to believe what I want to believe." Believing what we want to believe is a common but foolish desire. For example, I'd like to believe that eating cheeseburgers and ice cream while lounging on the couch would make me look like Arnold Schwarzenegger.

But my desire to believe that does not change reality. If I were my only resource for health and fitness, I would never become healthy.

The reality that governs how our body responds to our diet and level of activity is also called the natural law. Natural law, a preset, outside standard, often doesn't agree with our opinions or desires but always affects our well being.

Likewise we need outside standards in order to determine whether or not our self-esteem is substantiated.

The decision to ignore outside standards, specifically the natural law, can be deadly. Natural laws are those that cannot be refuted. No matter how badly we want to believe they do not apply to us, they do. For example, if I acted upon a sincere belief that I could breathe water rather than air, I would die. It would not matter how sincere my belief was.

This means we need to investigate what natural laws exist in the world and operate in concert with them. It doesn't mean we need to use *all* outside standards in order to determine our self-esteem. Obviously many individuals, groups, and organizations believe in different standards. We must determine which of these are consistent with natural law and our objectives in life before we decide to accept or reject them.

In other words we need to consider our standards *and* outside standards. Then we must look to see if these standards are in harmony with natural law. If they are, we can accept them and confidently know they will not come back to hurt our motivation or our self-esteem, or endanger our survival.

When explaining this topic, I once used the analogy that when we decide to fly a certain airline, we also decide to trust their standards. But when we walk down the jet way, if the aircraft we're supposed to board looks like a bathtub with plastic wings, the airline's obvious failure to understand the natural laws of flight would instantly destroy our confidence in them. As a result, we would reject the airline's standards because they were not in accordance with natural law.

A woman partially rejected my analogy, saying the Wright Brothers couldn't have invented flight without challenging the natural law.

"It's not natural for people to fly," she maintained. However, she was mistaken because the Wright Brothers were not trying to defy the natural law, they were trying to understand it. A greater understanding of the natural laws of gravity, the physics of thrust and lift, and the principles of controlling flight made flight possible. In other words submitting to the natural law and operating within its limits is what makes flight possible. Only when these laws are defied does an airplane crash.

Likewise in our daily lives, when we operate within the natural law we can discover new thrills, but if we defy it we will also crash.

The tough question is, how do we know what all of the natural laws are? This ultimately becomes a religious debate. While this book touches upon some aspects of faith, it was not written to provide a thorough explanation of the genesis of natural law. Although this information is not provided it's important to recognize the need to seek the truth and to abide by it once it has been found.

Self-esteem = Selfish-steam

As I grew up, I remember feeling terrible about my actions when they did not meet my parents' standards. That feeling motivated me to make changes so I could feel good about how I behaved. I never felt hopeless or unloved. I always knew that my parents had an unconditional love for me. However, my parents spent more time teaching me to be respectful of others than to be worrying about myself.

When we treat others with respect they have a tendency to treat us with respect also. Respect begets respect. As a result we have a sense of self-respect that sufficiently fills the need for self–esteem.

Is it any wonder that some teachers report that today's kids act with less respect for authority than in the past? Why not? We teach kids to regard themselves with higher esteem than anyone else in the world. We send them into the world, selfish. Filled with *selfish-steam*.

We should be doing just the opposite. We should teach them the value of standards, order, and discipline to function outside of self. They must be taught that serving and respecting others is honorable. How does this relate to you?

The answer is that we all go through stages in life in which we wear moral and/or logical blindfolds. It takes maturity, and wisdom gained through living, to unveil our ignorance. We can all relate to the feeling of embarrassed enlightenment we have all experienced when our ignorance was exposed. To elaborate on these blindfolds we all wear, let's look at a typical child.

An 18 month-old who cries when prevented from playing with a burning candle does not see the danger in the activity. No matter how we try to caution the child, he thinks being deprived of the fun is unfair.

In just a few short years, when the child is five years old, he can see the logic behind the decision—his blindfold has been removed. However, new blindfolds have replaced it. These new blindfolds prevent the child from seeing the reasons behind limiting his consumption of junk foods or setting a bedtime.

Life experience and a measure of maturity gained when the child is fifteen can make his old perspectives about bedtimes and junk food seem funny to him. His blindfolds on those issues have long been removed, but he now wears a new one. This blindfold covers up his understanding on why his parents won't let him go to a party on Saturday night. At this age it may seem more like this blindfold is stapled to his face rather than loosely tied to it. He, for the life of him, can not understand how his parents could possibly be so strict about a simple party. This blindfold may not be removed until he has his own 15-year-old son, but eventually as he matures it comes off.

The point is, we all wear blindfolds at one time or another. We may have one on right now. If we do not seek counsel from people other than ourselves we may never remove the blindfolds holding us back. Many times these blindfolds are very personal and include self-esteem-related issues. Sometimes the blindfolds that we wear prevent us from growing or changing our own behavior.

The packaging does not change the contents.

The accepted popularity of how to attain *self*-esteem mangles the moral fiber of our society. This warped perspective on *self*-esteem blurs the foundation for motivation. No matter how well people package self-esteem, the package holds selfishness.

Some people ask me, "Dave, if you're right about the overreliance of our culture on self-esteem, how did the topic become so popular?"

There are two primary reasons for this popularity. First, it's a seductive concept that people want to believe. Second, writers such as Dr. Branden state things like, "I cannot remember a time when I did not perceive this doctrine (re: "living for others," "obedience," and "selflessness") disastrous for mental and emotional well being."(pg. 148 How to Raise Your Self-Esteem).

Those opinions appeal to people. They validate our own selfishness. When people can reference a book, with a doctor's name on it, to bolster up their reasons for being selfish, they will. Some people claim that their selfishness is an honorable thing to pursue, in the name of their own well being. People who have bought into pop-culture's glorified self-esteem philosophy often defend it vehemently. That philosophy is their shield against being called selfish, and they know it.

Some psychologists claim a scientific connection between self-esteem and results. However, the variables they chose to include or omit affect—and in some cases have largely determined—the results of their studies. The same argument, of course, can be used to reject studies I find more credible. Nevertheless, numerous studies reveal few, if any, connections between focusing on self-esteem and results.

These studies demonstrate that focusing on self-esteem does not contribute to students' performance, cultural prosperity or job performance. One such study done by Professor Bruce Ryan at the University of Guelph shows that the effects of behaviors, for fourth through seventh graders, such as acting out, internalizing problems, peer sociability, and rule compliance were completely irrelevant to self-esteem. In a conversation I had with Professor Ryan, he exclaimed, "The most powerful factors for predicting academic success are intellectual effectiveness and academic effort."

On February 5th 1990, *Time Magazine* published an article about a standardized math test that was given to 13 year-olds in six different countries. The test included the statement "I am good at mathematics." The students were to answer yes or no as to whether or not that statement described them personally. The American students scored the worst on the math portion of the test but ranked the highest on the self-esteem related question. 68% of the American students felt they were good at math.

The philosophy of self-esteem has penetrated our society to an astonishing degree, as shown by the math study question. Our young people had the worst scores but the greatest self-esteem. They operate under a delusion, comical if it didn't indicate such dire consequences for both the individual students and our nation. Fostered by the philosophy of self-esteem, our young children believe a falsehood: if they think they're good at math, they are, regardless of their test results.

Even Dr. Branden, himself, would not classify these children as having healthy self-esteem. He commented on the *Time* article saying, "One of the characteristics of people with healthy self-esteem is that they tend to assess their abilities and accomplishments realistically, neither denying nor exaggerating them." (The Power of Self–Esteem, Dr. Branden Health Communications Inc. Page 34)

This is where the problem enters in again. How are these children supposed to assess their own "abilities or accomplishments" when they are told to disregard outside standards as well as people that make them feel bad? There's only one answer. They *must* consider the standards of others if they are to make an accurate assessment of themselves.

Union of Esteem

According to the National Center for Health Statistics, the divorce rate nearly doubled from mid 1960s to the mid 1990s. I find the correlation between the timing of the societal shift toward the importance of self-esteem and the divorce rate during the last half-century very interesting. To me the relationship is telling: The greater the focus on *self*, the higher the divorce rate.

Many marital problems stem from selfishness. The unfaithful person puts libido ahead of marriage. The person who uses financial problems as an excuse for divorce covets money over marriage.

There is little to no room to focus on self in marriage. Rather, a person must consider marriage a *union of esteem*. A union of esteem means loving the couple you become in marriage above yourself.

Think of the powerful symbol of lighting the Unity candle at a wedding. The bride and groom pick up two candles at the altar representing each individual. The flames are united into one larger one. Then, the couple extinguishes the individual candles, representing themselves.

I will never forget asking the priest, during the rehearsal for my own wedding, "Which side of the altar do I walk around after we light the Unity candle?"

"Dave, that's easy, you go where she goes," he answered. "From that point forward you are one!"

The most challenging time in our marriage came just after the birth of our first child. When Kevin arrived, we, as many new parents, felt stripped of every spare moment. I would come home from work and think, "I need a break." Lisa would see me come home from work and think she deserved a break. This was miserable. It was not until we put each other's needs first that we found peace and as a result, wonderful and powerful motivation.

> A person focused on "self" in marriage does not serve the marriage.

A person focused on "self" in marriage does not serve the marriage. If you come home from work like I did, tired and irritable, you too may feel as though you deserve a break. But in reality, your spouse may have had an even worse day. If you are focused on yourself, your spouse may not have the opportunity to share with you his or her own situation. If the kids need your help, the bills need to be paid and your in-laws are coming for a visit next

week, tension can rise and resentment can build.

This is when people start feeling sorry for themselves. It's also when we get nit-picky about who has done what. "I did the dishes last night, you should do them tonight." or "Can't you just ONE time help get the kids in bed?" Soon we start keeping track of points and the focus that we have on ourselves reduces us to the behavior of an overtired three year-old.

On the other hand, a couple focusing on serving the marriage as a unit attends to each other. The desire for service to one's self disappears. When one partner needs the support of the other, the other partner pitches in to help. A union of esteem evolves.

Too often so-called marriage counselors take a what-are-you-being-deprived-of approach to counseling couples. This is like helping the couple fill out divorce papers.

Too often so-called marriage counselors take a "what-are-you-being-deprived-of," approach to counseling couples. This is like helping the couple fill out divorce papers. If you focus on yourself you will never be satisfied. The effective solution gets the marriage partners focused on serving each other, which is rewarding in two ways. First, the feeling a person gets from willfully doing for others is incredible. Second, when two people serve each other, two people also receive a service. Therefore they no longer feel needy.

A misplaced desire for self-esteem destroys the purity of motivation. Even major league baseball suffers from runaway self-esteem. Team loyalty plays the victim. Today, free agency helps players get the most money year after year, placing the focus on the individual, not on the team. Self-loyalty replaces fan loyalty, coach loyalty, and town loyalty. Unfortunately, the nature of the game changes because many players measure their self-esteem by the size of a their contract.

As I mentioned earlier, companies also suffer the cost of rampant self-esteem. If an employee needs daily assurance that he or she is the greatest and doesn't get his daily pat, he plans to quit and look for appreciation and praise elsewhere.

It's okay to *like* recognition as an employee. However, employees who *need* recognition all the time, usually don't become legacy achievers. In fact, self-esteem-driven employees often self-destruct. No one prospers from the *appreciate-me-or-I-quit* attitude.

That outward philosophy holds true for people in leadership roles, too. Leaders preoccupied with self-esteem inevitably make decisions motivated by selfish agendas. Selfish agendas hurt the organization.

Suppose Phil Jackson, coach of the incomparable Chicago Bulls during the 1990s, craved more personal glory for the team's success than Michael Jordan was receiving.

Think of the destructive moves the coach could have made if his focus was on himself instead of the team. Yet, Phil Jackson shined the light on Michael and other Bulls to create a cohesive team—a team that responded to the coach.

An indescribable feeling of exhilaration comes from putting others first. Life gets easier when you focus on family, friends, church, vocation, and others instead of self.

This philosophy may sound very contrary to popular books that push selfish concepts including the best seller "Looking Out for #1." This book mocks the idea of putting others first. Yet, I challenge you to find a happy, successful person whose main focus is building self-esteem or focusing on self.

After all, the greatest way to diminish your ability to motivate yourself is to focus on yourself.

The entertainment industry is loaded with successful people who need alcohol or drugs to get through the night. As a result, many of today's stars are killing themselves with drug overdoses or alcoholism. Years ago, two of the most famous actors of their time, William Holden and Richard Burton, succumbed to alcohol. More recently, John Belushi and Chris Farley used the same combination of cocaine and morphine to accidentally end their lives, both at age 33. The number of similar cases in the entertainment industry is too long to list here.

Yet there are also many exceptions. Michael Caine won't shoot a film on location unless his family can be with him so he can make sure they are safe and comfortable. Celine Dion and her husband, after battling his cancer into remission together, renewed their marriage vows. Then, at the pinnacle of her success, she has temporarily retired to spend more time with him and realize her hopes for children.

Paul Newman, who was also troubled by the realities of celebrity, found better ways than drugs to come to terms with fame and riches. He used his name-recognition to build a highly successful food company whose entire after-tax profits go to charities. Since some aspects of celebrity made Newman uncomfortable—especially its tendency to exalt the self-esteem of the recipient—he focused its power on others through his food company and his charities. Celebrities who

Ironically, what people gain by focusing on others instead of themselves is exactly what people focused on building self-esteem crave, but never get.

lack this moral foundation often ask themselves, "Is this all there is?" and drift into searching for more in destructive ways.

Ironically, what people gain by focusing on others instead of themselves is exactly what people focused on building self-esteem crave but never get.

The Eye of the Beholder— Self-esteem and Appearance

As said before, self-esteem can't be determined solely by our own independent standards. But this doesn't mean I believe our personal opinions don't have a role in determining how we feel about ourselves. They do. What people say about us often influences how we feel about ourselves. If a young person is told they're ugly by someone they respect, they may start believing it. This is sad and can have a brutal effect on their perception of themselves.

Yet some people who are told they're beautiful by someone they respect, still insist they are not. In fact to themselves their personal appearance may really be distressing. Ugly and beautiful are matters of taste. If a person's taste happens to conflict with their own personal physical appearance, they can't be convinced they have an attractive physical appearance.

It's a mistake to tell them they must see themselves as being physically beautiful. This will press them to spend excessive time examining their personal appearance, something they have already decided is ugly.

Focusing on unchangeable things we don't like about ourselves—such as our height, facial shape, or bone structure—is futile. Rather, focusing on things that we can change about ourselves makes more sense. Obviously, we can change some of our physical attributes such as hairstyle, and even our weight to a certain degree.

I know people who are convinced they are ugly and yet they have high self-esteem. I have also known people who are convinced they are physically beautiful, yet have low self-esteem. Logically speaking, the only conclusion to these observations is that our appearance is not the deciding factor in our self-esteem.

We have all seen television commercials promising to restore your hair "but more importantly your self-esteem." Does loss of hair equate to a loss of self-esteem? Certainly not to all bald men. In fact, Michael Jordan chose to shave his head to appear bald. I doubt that he was deciding to remove his self-esteem.

If we try to convince someone they are physically beautiful when they don't believe they are, we will never win. Think of your own experiences in trying to do so. Sometimes we can't even convince them that we think they are beautiful. Trying to get a person to believe they are beautiful when they are simply not aesthetically wired to see it will not work. This is like trying to convince someone who doesn't like liver that it's a taste treat. No matter how many times they try it, they still don't like it. No mirror pep talk can change the reality. There is only one choice for a person in this situation: focus on outside factors rather than on oneself.

In high school I had an acne problem. This was something I thought was ugly. No one on the planet then or now could convince me otherwise. When I thought about my acne I wanted to shut down socially. In other words I would lose my motivation. When I took the focus off of my face and put it on the activities I was doing or on the people I was with, my personality would change. I became more confident and outgoing.

Taking the focus off myself was the solution to my self-esteem. In other words I did not look in the mirror and try to convince myself that I liked my appearance. I did not say, "I am a handsome young man" twenty times each morning in order to convince myself that I was wrong about my taste in looks. I just stopped focusing on what I could not change.

Does all this talk about serving others mean we don't spend any time on ourselves?

Certainly not. To do so would be neglecting ourselves, which would make us ineffective at serving those around us.

Obviously, there are times when we must invest in our attitudes and abilities or just take time for ourselves. To enhance our motivation, the investments we make in ourselves must be motivated by the right causes.

For example Brett Favre, long-time quarterback of the Green Bay Packers and three times the National Football League's Most Valuable Player, works hard at developing his throwing arm. He watches his diet, and studies game films. He is investing in himself and both he and the team benefit. And by maintaining and further developing his individual skills, he fulfills his obligation to serve the team.

If his motivation to do this were only to glorify himself or to secure a better contract, he would cloud his motivation

and it would hurt his performance as well as the team's results. In the same way a paramedic is not being selfish when he or she spends extra time learning better life saving techniques. This is an investment in time for the good of others. A paramedic could even justify taking a break from the action to go golfing as a means to refocus. None of this is selfish if it is done for the right reasons.

Likewise, a mother can justify a night out with the ladies as a means to relax in order to refocus on her family. We all need to take some time to develop our own attitudes or just plain relax in order to be effective. We just need to pay close attention to our purpose for doing so.

~~~

"We must be courageous but also reasonable. The world admires us for walking a tightrope without falling off. It asks us to keep our balance."

—— Lech Walesa

Chapter 2

The Pursuit of Life's Perfect Balance

Balance in life generates motivation, leading directly to success. This conviction comes both from my research and my heart.

The topics of motivation and life balance are very personal to me. Like all of us, I am pulled in many different directions every day. Therefore, a major benefit of researching and writing this book has been the opportunity to test my own motivation as well as practice my balance skills.

I try to live in the manner presented in these pages—the key word being *try*. In pursuit of this goal I continuously work to improve my own life despite setbacks and failures ranging from mildly disappointing to severely painful. Ultimately, however, every setback and failure I experience equips me with greater motivational skills. Knowing this helps me minimize the damage of every crisis and get through it quicker.

Whether you consider yourself highly motivated or highly unmotivated, you will be able to better your life through the examples set for us by legacy achievers.

Motivation results from the successful pursuit of life's perfect balance. So what is *balance*? Webster defines balance as *mental or emotional stability*.

In order to feel mentally and emotionally stable in life, we need to balance six significant points. Whether or not their presence or absence is recognized, everyone's life needs these six balance points. There are many other aspects of life, but none are as important as the six. Legacy achievers focus on them.

The Six Balance Points

- ~ Family
- ~ Financial Responsibility
- ~ Health
- ~ Social Contribution
- ~ Education/Vocation: *Knowledge in Motion*
- ~ Faith

Balance is Engaging

Balance is not about avoidance. Balance is about engaging in a pursuit, and meeting challenges rather than dodging them. Often the worst response we can make in a situation is to do nothing.

Some people may try to balance their health by avoiding fat-laden foods and sugar, but if they don't exercise, the consumption of healthy food alone is not going to make them healthy.

Some people might say, "I want to get my life in balance by spending more time with my family." So they spend more time at home with their family, but all they do is watch television. To pursue life's perfect balance, we need to engage in activities that bring our family closer together. This can be as simple and cost-free as going outside and playing catch with your children, or as complicated and expensive as taking your family skiing, sailing, or rafting down the Colorado River.

Some people decide, "I need to get in balance financially, so I'm going to clip coupons." But they are not in balance unless they invest wisely enough to make their money grow.

Thus, the pursuit of balance has two aspects: the negative and the positive. The positive element—taking action—is the most important for most people. The negative element—avoiding certain things—is somewhat less important except to people who are fighting an addiction of some sort. To them, avoidance of their particular poison is one of the most positive things they can do.

Balance Equals Energy, Effort, and Focus

To gain life's balance, we cannot merely divide 24 hours a day by the six balance points. Gaining balance is not just about time. It's about energy. It's about effort. It's about focus.

Even if we need to work ten hours a day, with energy, effort, and focus we can still sustain balance by pulling harder on the other balance points to make sure things even out. Maintaining balance takes energy and contemplation, but the effort pays off in peace of mind. Conversely, if we fall off balance every other part of our life suffers.

Spinning the plates

Life balance is like a performer spinning plates at the circus. He puts a plate on a long stick and spins it, balancing it as he sets up another stick and spins a second plate. He adds another and another.

How many plates can he spin at one time? Think of your own life. The balance points in life are like having six plates to spin. Our six plates are family, finances, health, social contribution, education/vocation, and faith. Just like the circus performer, we need to continually give each plate at least a little attention—at least a little tweak—to keep it spinning smoothly.

Life balance is like a performer spinning plates at the circus.

If we have only one focus in life—probably on our ambitions and career—it may consume most of our time and energy. We might find ourselves thinking along these lines: "To be brutally honest, I like this plate a lot more than any of the others, so I'm just going to keep on spinning it, and let the others take care of themselves."

For a short time the other plates may keep spinning on their momentum, but if ignored for a long time they will begin to wobble. Sooner or later they'll fall, usually sooner than we expect. When the ignored plates fall with a crash, so does our life.

Spinning plates provides a powerful visual image of the focus and effort we need to put into each of life's balance points. This image also makes it easy to see how it works: if we neglect any given plate, it wobbles and eventually falls. When a plate falls, it breaks. The broken plate provides a readily understandable picture of an out-of-balance life. It could represent a broken marriage or being broke financially. When this happens, we need to glue the pieces back together.

However, when we repair a broken plate, it's vital to make sure we don't neglect the other spinning plates or they will fall too. It's far easier to keep all six spinning than it is to keep five spinning while we repair one. Let two or three plates fall, and the difficulties can seem insurmountable. But the repair task is never impossible—it will simply take longer and demand greater effort.

The solution to regaining balance is to engage energy, effort, and focus together. Our problem may lie in not understanding how little time it can take—if the time is used sincerely, thoughtfully, and energetically—to maintain spin on any of the plates we're tempted to neglect.

To maintain balance, we need to educate ourselves about all six of the balance points. We need to study how we can keep them all spinning in our present circumstances. We need to attend to each of the balance points each day, and give each one anything from a quick twirl to heavy attention. This is the inescapable necessity and joy of living a satisfying, highly motivated, balanced life.

The best part is, it doesn't feel overwhelming when you get in the habit of always giving all six of the balance points a little tweak, a little added spin, every day. Only when we let some of the plates—or even just one of them—start to wobble and fall, do we really feel overwhelmed and out of control.

You may see the six points and say, "Hey, you forgot golf." Spending time on hobbies and personal interests before balancing the relevant points in life is an easy trap to fall into. You may even say, "Why do you want to impose your personal viewpoints on me? Golf (or whatever) is really important to my vision of life."

This is a gross misunderstanding of balance for two important reasons: First, the concepts I present go well beyond my own opinions. In fact, my opinions were shaped by my studies of legacy achievers—what they focus on and how they keep their lives in balance. Putting your participation in golf or some other pastime ahead of life-balancing points inevitably disrupts balance. As your out-of-balance life wobbles, your friendships, family, and career begin to suffer.

My point is not that golf kills, although sometimes it feels like it does to me personally. Rather, favoring priorities outside the six balance points usually ends in disaster. We may coast through life out of balance for some time, but eventually plates start to fall. Then we are left with nothing but broken pieces.

The second reason is that balanced people find great joy in hobbies such as golf or just plain goofing off. When our lives are in balance, we actually find more time to enjoy other activities than when we are out of balance. In fact, mixing hobbies and other favorite activities into our balance points becomes incredibly rewarding.

We need to educate ourselves in order to understand the real value of the six balance points. We need to know how they work together. If we concentrate on balance every day we will generate motivation, and it will guide us to success.

Of course, some days we can't be present to spin all the plates. If you travel all day, it may be impossible to spend time with your children or with your spouse—but, chances are—you can phone home. With cellular phones, what could be easier?

Maybe you can't be there for your daughter's dance recital. When something like this happens, you need to twirl the family plate harder to move back into balance again. The key point here is to know how long you can travel before you lose the ability and strength to balance what is currently out of balance.

A closer look at each balance point

Family ~

Today's technology allows us to get things done faster, go places quicker, and communicate better than ever before. Yet families are also more out of touch than ever before.

The family dinner has been replaced by the fast-food drive through on the way to soccer practice. Live, in-person, role models have been replaced by fictitious television characters with oversexed and easily outclassed personalities.

The number of sensible parents who monitor what their children watch on TV has been overtaken by the number of parents who let the tail wag the dog at home. They justify letting their pre-teen children watch violence and sexually explicit content by saying, "What are we to do? They happen to like it."

For many of our middle-class citizens, the American Dream once meant having a white picket fence around a home filled with two loving spouses and happy, well-mannered children. But for many today, the old American Dream has been replaced by today's reality: a security fence around a massive house half-filled by what's left of a broken or dysfunctional family, its rooms stuffed with expensive status-displaying gadgets.

This is the sad picture of many American households today, and a major part of the problem is the growing lack of balance in our culture. When we put our work and finances ahead of our families, we do grave damage to ourselves as well as to the people around us. The ramifications of such a tragic lack of balance destroy our ability to focus. This in turn destroys our ability to be motivated and eventually ends in disaster.

Understanding how to balance the important responsibilities we each have to our family, along with the rest of our non-work lives, is crucial to our well being. We can find abundant joy in our family relationships, and they can be a source of true motivation.

Although we are talking about family, it's important to remember that each of the balance points has an effect on the others. For example, if parents neglect to discipline their child—when the youngster's behavior cries out for discipline—and continue this neglect for a long time, they can be sure of what will happen. The child will grow into an undisciplined young adult who will get into serious trouble as a direct result of not being adequately disciplined when small.

When trouble of this kind comes calling, the parents are forced to respond. Depending on the situation, the stress could lead to difficulty in concentrating at work. The challenges at work are likely to have a financial impact on the family. To handle the stress, the parent might exercise less and eat more. The resulting tension could lead to neglect of societal responsibilities. While all of these worldly matters are tearing at one's heart and mind, the person under stress may forget to ask for God's help. As a result, all of the balance points fall victim to the original problem, which was neglecting family responsibilities.

This is why we need to keep a shared focus on each of the balance points. Thankfully, a simple awareness of the six balance points is often all many people need to get started toward leading a balanced life. For others it takes a bit more.

We can learn a lot from two very important lessons taught by legacy achievers: First, a legacy achiever puts his or her family ahead of self. Second, legacy achievers look at families as *no wimp clubs*.

Putting Family First

Let's carry the philosophy I shared in the previous chapter further. When a family reaches the threshold of unbalance, the result can be divorce. Although not a positive topic for discussion, we can learn how to avoid this tragedy by looking at its cause.

Divorces are caused by selfishness.

That may sound like a personal judgment but it's not. Rather, it's a conclusion derived from talking to a large number of divorcees of both genders who have shared their stories. According to all of them, when they cut through the froth to the basic reason, selfishness caused their marriages to break up.

Further examination divided them into three groups: the majority blame their ex-spouse's selfishness, a smaller group say they were both selfish, and even fewer admit the breakup was caused primarily by their own selfishness. When we break down the trigger causes for divorce, it's easier to see this.

The unfaithful person puts sexual desire ahead of the marriage. A couple divorcing for financial reasons puts material goods, services or addictions ahead of family. The couples claiming to have fallen out of love selfishly stopped loving. Spousal abuse is caused by a selfish need for control or a selfish lack of control over temper. The workaholic selfishly puts his or her career ahead of family.

Even more subtle reasons for divorce are forms of selfishness. For example, communicating ineffectively can be a lack of willingness to learn about the other person, which is essentially a selfish attitude.

This is not to say these things aren't difficult to handle—they are. I'm familiar with the stress financial constraints can put on a marriage. At age 24, I ran into a financial struggle as a result of being self-employed, which meant it could happen again the following year. My financial obligations included tens of thousands of dollars in short term debt—plus car and mortgage payments—all piled up in one year.

Lisa was not earning an income because she was staying home with our son, Kevin. To complicate matters, we were expecting our second child and did not have a maternity rider on our health insurance policy. Our insurance company refused the rider because Lisa's first delivery was a C-section, which cost them $23,000. This meant we personally faced the possibility of additional hospital bills totaling the same amount. Adding to the stress, I had to work harder than normal to make up the funds. It was a tough year. We went through a lot of aspirin.

When I look back on our difficult year, I can see how being challenged by finances can hurt a relationship. But I can also see how those challenges create an opportunity to grow as a family. Lisa and I took the opportunity to reaffirm the commitments we made to each other before we married. Due to our own positive childhood experiences, we decided we would live in a tent and ride bikes before we would send our children to daycare. We actually used those words to paint the picture of the priority in our lives prior to our wedding. When the financial strain hit, the unwanted challenge was an opportunity to stay true to our commitment. The whole situation, because of balance, became a positive experience in our lives.

Taking the focus off ourselves and putting it on the needs of our children provided a sense of security. Knowing what was really important to us allowed me to focus on my responsibilities to the family as well as Lisa to concentrate on hers. With our perseverance and pursuit of balance including faith in God, we were able to conquer the financial challenge in the following months and years.

To many people, divorce is not a concern. The commitment to their vows—for richer or poorer, for better or worse, in sickness and in health—never wavers. To these people, the challenge may be in finding happiness in the marriage to which they have committed. Couples throughout the world who have found happiness, discovered it by serving the members of their family. These people have discovered the value of taking the focus off themselves and putting it on others. Through their unselfishness, they actually receive more from their families than do selfish individuals who try to get the family to focus on them.

Some people get nervous when they hear about legacy achievers putting their families first. They feel as though such an attitude might compromise their work performance. But, as we mentioned earlier, legacy achievers are the employees that companies pursue. They have their personal life in order and as a result can concentrate effectively and creatively at work. They register fewer sick days and can even put in overtime when necessary because they don't have to worry about plates falling around them.

A person who routinely neglects family responsibility is put under tremendous pressure when they need to commit extra hours at work. The decision to stay longer at work may mean a long-unspun plate will fall. When out-of-balance people are asked to work overtime, they face a much bigger decision than does a legacy achiever. The unbalanced person, to a degree, is forced to choose between family and work.

A Happy Family is a No Wimps Club

With privileges come responsibilities, as every legacy achiever understands. Meeting responsibilities involves sacrifices. Making sacrifices means no wimping out. In marriage, we must be willing to face its difficulties; they are part of the marriage. Abandoning the problem is not a solution. It simply creates a greater problem. When our children are disobedient, it takes effort to discipline them. But failure to discipline them always creates even greater problems.

Too often these days, parents are afraid to discipline their children. This fear leads to a lack of balance in the lives of every family member.

It begins when the children are very young. A young toddler is given whatever he wants because he creates a very loud scene if he isn't. Faced with the fear of a scene, the parents cave in and give the child whatever he wants.

When the child is older, bigger, and louder, the fear in the parent will escalate. And, because the youngster has been trained to believe he can get everything he wants simply by being nasty, he will be almost impossible to please.

No doubt about it, there are valid reasons to fear children. Lisa and I have four children and hope for more. Having a martial arts background, I have been in the ring against men as large as 6'5" and 309 lbs. None of them had the chutzpa my four-year-old son has. At the moment he stands about 2' 10" high and weighs 38 pounds, but he has more drive in him than any ten of those men.

His commitment to get what he wants is amazing. When he was three years old he went through a bad phase including throwing cereal bowls and temper tantrums lasting as long as an hour at decibel levels that would have made The Who wear ear plugs.

The situation called for an intense commitment from mom and dad to correct his actions. Not having gone through this with our other children, Lisa and I wondered where we had gone wrong.

When my parents witnessed his temperament, they didn't respond with the same concern we felt. In fact, they laughed!

My mom said, "Dave, now you know exactly how you acted when you were three years old." They then provided counsel on how to correct the problem.

With our improved perspective, Lisa and I set out on an intense corrective program. We had to be brave enough, and persistent enough, to address every single rebellious action. It also demanded plenty of energy for the essential follow-through. Envisioning our child twice as large and twice as loud was some inspiration to stay committed. But the thought of how miserable his life would be if he did not learn to control himself was the real motivation behind our determination to control his defiance. Thankfully, our son has moved past this behavior and although he occasionally tests the old behavior, he quickly realizes his objectionable actions get him nowhere. Today he controls his emotions much better and, as he has always done, makes me smile every day.

A husband who feels that he needs to improve his communication with his wife must be brave enough to deal with the reality. The wife who feels she needs to fix everything about her husband must also be courageous in letting go of this common obsession. Children must also face responsibility. They must be brave in disclosing the truth to their parents about the mistakes they have made.

All these factors add up to one thing. Families are "No Wimps Clubs." Remember, balance is about engaging in actions; it doesn't come from avoiding difficult situations. To find balance the fearful parents, the husband who lacks communication skills, the wife who feels she's married to a fixer-upper sort of husband, and the demanding children all need to engage in thoughts or actions requiring courage.

Sometimes we need to make tough choices. If the choice compromises our family's well-being, we have made the wrong one. If it serves our family, we will never regret it.

We must remain strong and build courage to handle the difficulties of life. This is not always easy to do, especially when we are faced with 36 hours worth of things to do in a 24 hour day.

Sometimes we need to make tough choices. If the choice compromises our family's well-being, we have made the wrong one. If it serves our family, we will never regret it.

Finances ~

Taking money with you isn't nearly as important as making it last until you're ready to go.

—— Anonymous

Financial responsibility means something different to each of us. We often associate money with emotions. Some people experience varied levels of self-esteem, happiness, sadness, jealousy, greed, generosity, distress, excitement, failure, and success all due to money-related matters. Money can generate an equal number of positive and negative emotions.

Sometimes the idea of balancing our finances can be overwhelming. Our society sends us so many mixed messages about money. Some people live by this philosophy: since you can't take it with you, you might just as well spend it as fast as you get it. Others, suffering from an even greater lack of self-control, take it a step further and spend money before they earn it. In contrast, others go to the opposite extreme and hoard money as a means of security.

What is the favorable perspective to have on how we handle our wealth? Legacy achievers have a tremendous perspective on money and, not surprisingly, their perspective is balanced. Legacy achievers enjoy a portion of their money today while they save some for tomorrow. All the while they give to worthy causes. But money is not the only way legacy achievers measure earthly wealth. Time, talent, and relationships are priceless assets.

I gained a great perspective about money from a legacy achiever named Marty Domitrovich. He said, "money is only good for the good it does." This attitude is commonplace in the lives of most legacy achievers. A story he told me about himself illustrated that he meant what he said. Marty met his wife, Katie, in the late 1960's when he worked as an in-the-home knife, pot and pan salesperson. Katie's father liked Marty but objected strenuously to his daughter marrying a "door to door knife salesman."

Katie's father even refused to go to the wedding because he did not approve a marriage "doomed to be burdened by financial ruin," as he put it. This upset Marty and Katie very much. Marty was so filled with negative feelings for his father-in-law that he knew nothing good would come of his thoughts. He knew he had to turn the negative emotions into something constructive for the good of his family.

He privately made a commitment to himself to earn enough money in the knife business to donate more to a charity than his father-in-law made in a full year.

A number of years later Marty made good on his promise and donated the money. I'll never forget the feeling of accomplishment in his voice when he told me this story. But he never told his father-in-law, nor did he strain the relationship by holding a grudge. This constructive goal allowed less fortunate people to benefit from what was initially a negative circumstance.

Legacy achievers do not view being rich or being poor as either good or bad. Rather, they look at the way people handle their money as a measure of their character.

The careers some legacy achievers choose are not lucrative. These people demonstrate their character and maturity by living within their means and, despite not having a lot of money, still contribute their time and talent to other worthy causes.

Many legacy achievers with more financial flexibility are careful to keep materialism at bay. They are conscious that money itself is okay but, "the love of money is a root of all kinds of evil." (1 Timothy 6:10 NIV)

In order to keep our lives in balance we need to balance our finances. When we experience financial pressures, our judgment can become clouded. It's important to become educated about money and engage in actions that will allow us to help ourselves and others financially.

Health ~ 🐛🐛🐛

Good health is something that makes you feel
it's a fine day when it isn't.
— Anonymous

Legacy achievers are motivated to stay healthy because of the impact their ill-health would have on others who are close to them. If our health were to fail, it would put tremendous burdens on our family and others who care about us. Life deals enough challenges without our neglect helping it along. Therefore it makes sense for us to avoid

tragedy or careless health habits whenever possible. Healthy choices are a great way to do this.

Just as neglecting our family and our finances can have a domino effect on other balance points, so too can our health. Balancing our health and well being can be both complicated and simple. Complicated because we are constantly bombarded with sales pitches regarding good health that appeal to our egos and any tempting hedonistic impulses we may harbor. Simple because some basic principles have passed the test of time and are readily available for our use.

First, we must acknowledge that we will never find the key to better health exclusively ...

...in a fad diet

...by eating only what are now considered healthy foods

...by just going to the gym or running

...by just taking vitamins or supplements

These are fleeting, one-dimensional solutions. A relatively healthy person will only find the key to good health by combining the following four things: **reasonable diet, routine exercise, controlled stress, and monitored risks.**

Reasonable Diet

Every so often a new weight reduction philosophy takes America by storm. During the 1960s, the popular solution was to avoid starches. In the 1970s, avoiding sugar was stressed. During the 1980s and 90s, avoiding fat was pounded into our minds. A current craze is the Atkin's diet which, though known for years, recently gained more popularity. This diet does not restrict fat, but limits carbohydrates.

You can find people who claim each of these fad diets is the be all and end all answer to good health. You can also find people who claim to have tried these diets and say they don't work.

Most people who live long healthy lives do not stay committed to these extreme diets. Rather, they eat reasonably throughout their lives. The problem with most of us today is we are looking for the magic solution to great health as long as it's effortless.

Routine Exercise

Eating properly alone won't give us healthy balance. A study published by the American Journal of Clinical Nutrition showed that 90 percent of people who lose weight and keep it off also exercise at least 30 minutes four times a week.

The Institute for Aerobics Research in Dallas, Texas, found that people who don't exercise have poorer attitudes toward food than do people who exercise. Sedentary people tend to think healthy food is boring, difficult to find, and too time consuming. However, adopting healthy eating habits, when combined with adequate exercise, will improve our attitude about food. A good attitude enhances motivation.

Exercise may also reduce the odds of developing deadly diseases including heart-related problems and cancer. Some studies indicate that athletes are more than 50 percent less likely to develop certain diseases than non-athletes. A report published in The New England Journal of Medicine relates that middle-aged men reduce the risk of developing diabetes by six percent for every 500 calories burned by exercising weekly.

Exercise is also the most significant way to slow the aging process. Our bodies contain a substance called Human Growth Hormone (HGH). Once we reach our twenties, naturally released amounts of HGH start to decline. Scientists say that reversing the aging process requires the release of more HGH. Exercise does this. When you exercise, natural HGH pours into your system, which probably explains why many people who work out look younger than their counterparts who don't exercise.

Controlling Stress

A third major health factor is controlling stress. Excess stress may cause tremendous physical and emotional health problems. Both appropriate diet and exercise help control stress, but you can do more. Consider the following two commonalties among legacy achievers when it comes to handling stress.

1. Get Enough Sleep

Easy tasks are hard to handle when you're tired. Sometimes we refuse to admit we're tired. This may be a carryover from childhood. When, late in the day children become crabby, parents know they're simply tired, although the children will deny it emphatically.

Adults often have the same reaction to fatigue. We also become crabby. Unfortunately, we are a lot bigger and a lot louder and no one can make us go to bed.

2. Face the Problems

Another good way to reduce stress is to face our problems head on. This of course is consistent with engaging in action as opposed to avoidance in order to find balance.

Researchers at Southern Methodist University in Dallas believe we can improve our immune system and increase our sense of well-being by taking the time to actually write down our worries. Writing down worries helps because problems become more tangible and thus more controllable.

This activity allows us to view and understand problems in a concrete manner.

The general nature of the relationship between stress and illness has long been known to the medical world. Some doctors believe stress and feeling a loss of control may double our chance of catching the common cold because these emotions can reduce the effectiveness of the immune system. Therefore, facing our problems is extremely important in controlling stress.

3. Monitor Risks

Physical activities sometimes expose us to risks, therefore we should carefully calculate what we choose to do and the consequences we may face as a result of our choices. However, at the same time we can't live in total fear, and refuse to take part in any activity which presents some risk. We must simply think ahead and take precautions in order to guard our physical health.

If we were to live in constant fear of being hurt, we would most assuredly miss out on some great pleasures in life. Unfortunately, many things can cause us to fear activities. For example, horseback riding accidents put 70,000 people a year in the hospital. It's enough to scare some people away from ever getting on a horse. But an isolated statistic may not tell the entire story. It's wise to find out all the facts before we choose to participate in or avoid life's pleasures.

Bowling injuries cause 22,000 people a year to seek medical treatment. This news probably won't keep you out of the alleys if you enjoy bowling. However this statistic can put horseback riding injuries into perspective.

We can not be effective in life if we live with excessive fear of risk. Likewise, we cannot be effective if we throw all caution to the wind. Once again the secret lies in how we

balance our risks. We need to consider more than ourselves when we calculate what activities we choose. This means carefully considering who is affected by the state of our health.

Social Contributions ~

Do something for somebody everyday
for which you do not get paid.

—— Albert Schweitzer

There seems to be a growing *what's-in-it-for-me* attitude in America today. Proof of this being a very popular attitude is illustrated by heavy sales of a book titled *Looking Out For Number #1*.

It was a best seller for over a year, and still, long after its release, is in demand. This book, which mocks the idea of helping others, almost literally flew of the bookshelves. For those of you who don't know, books sell mostly by word of mouth, which means many people loved the I—*Me* concept in *Looking Out for #1*, and couldn't wait to tell their friends about it.

The author, Robert J. Ringer, is articulate, intelligent, and witty. He says people do things in their own best interest. This is generally true.

However, it's not absolute. The fact that people often do things for their own best interest does not mean the practice is good. In reality, it's often destructive and can be a sign of weakness. When we overcome this weakness we will strengthen our society enormously.

Their seems to be a growing *what's-in-it-for-me* attitude in America today.

Ringer believes the opposite. He denies that people should ever do anything from which they derive no direct benefit. When a person does give without expecting anything in return, he believes they are acting irrationally.

On page 88 he says, "Simply stated, don't do something for the reason that it's 'the right thing to do' if there is no benefit to be derived from it." This concept completely disregards the scriptural teaching to give without expecting anything in return.

Do you suppose the people who recommended his book to their friends ever stopped to reflect on what kind of friend endorses such a concept? What would happen if your friends all bought into this concept on your moving day? What about when you get sick, need a ride to the airport, or just need someone to talk to?

Ringer goes well beyond preaching the importance of selfishness. He claims your standards should not be influenced by anyone but yourself. This of course is right in line with many of the self-esteem-related issues we discussed in Chapter 1. He actually says there is no such thing as a moral right or wrong. "Your moral standards should be what you define them to be." He goes on to say, "just make sure *your head is on straight*." (Page 56. Emphasis added.)

How do we know our head is on straight if we have nothing with which to compare its alignment? Ringer calls people who believe in natural law, in other words, people who believe in right and wrong, moral absolutists.

Ringer holds these people in such low regard, he actually categorizes them with violent criminals (page 70) thus leading us to suspect he nurses some serious hangovers from childhood, or is simply aiming for shock effect.

He also expresses low regard for rapists, murderers, and robbers, apparently not realizing how ironic this stance is.

After all, violent criminals are only following his advice by determining their own moral code and looking out for #1.

The most impressive companies I have worked with or interacted with have an attitude that is the complete opposite of looking out for #1. During a stay at Walt Disney World Yacht and Beach Club Resort for a convention, I had an opportunity to witness many selfless acts done by the staff there. I'm not talking about things the staff would be recognized for. I'm talking about social contributions being brought in to the work place.

In one instance I walked down what seemed like a hundred-yard-long hallway searching for the men's room. I must have looked somewhat confused as I had no idea where it was located. A gentleman vacuuming the carpet about forty yards away recognized my confusion, stopped what he was doing, walked down the hall, and pointed me in the right direction. He had nothing to gain by his actions and I had never even asked for his help. No supervisor was in sight and he set himself behind a few moments in his own duties. His small act of thoughtfulness is commonplace in Disney.

During the same convention I was the leadoff speaker at 9:00 a.m. My assistant and I had some puzzlement about some of the information called for in my presentation. I needed to run back to my room five minutes before I went on stage. However, my room was located about ten minutes away by foot.

As I ran from the meeting room, I saw a gentleman transporting laundry on a golf cart. I was about to explain my situation to him, hoping to get a ride. But before I could get past, "I'm in a hurry," he pulled me into the cart and whisked me away to my room. In fact, he even took me through restricted back ways, saying, "Don't tell anyone I took you through here because customers are not allowed to see this area."

He had nothing to gain from me or from any of his superiors. His social contribution along with the gentleman who helped me find the men's room were small examples of selflessness adding up to a mountain of service at Disney. If we could bring this attitude of social contribution into the workplace, onto the streets, and everywhere else in life, we would live in a wonderfully different world.

I don't want to live in a society where everyone is focused on looking out for # 1. We all need help at some point in our lives. For some of us it's in the form of money, time, or emotional support. Some days we help others because we know we are going to get something in return. But there are other times when we should give of ourselves without any strings attached. Sure we may get something in return but if we do, we should consider it simply a blessing and be grateful for it.

Our societal contributions go way beyond what we traditionally consider charities. The little things that we do each day add up and shape what we believe to be acceptable behavior.

For example, drunk driving statistics reflect the power of society's shifting views. Since 1982, fatalities related to drunk driving have fallen by 36% according to the MADD (Mothers Against Drunk Driving) web site.

In considerable part, this is due to the initial efforts of one person, Candy Lightner. Candy's daughter, while walking along a city street, was killed by a drunk driver. Because of her motherly pain, Candy helped found MADD. This organization's impact on the way we as a society view drunk driving has been incredibly effective and beneficial. Legislatures all across the United States have taken dramatic steps to discourage drunk driving because society now demands it.

It doesn't always take a large scale contribution to society like Candy Lightner's to make a difference. The way we treat the checkout clerk, waitress, or the driver who cuts us off on our way to work all add up too. In each instance, each of us is a part of the problem as well as part of the solution. If we want to change the world we must begin by changing our own attitudes.

> If we want to change the world we must begin by changing our own attitudes.

Education/Vocation/Career (Knowledge in Motion) ~

> *I don't think much of a man who is not wiser today than he was yesterday.*
>
> .—— Abraham Lincoln

One of the first mentors I had as a businessperson is a man named Don Freda. He is a successful leader and was the founder of a very successful company. It was his responsibility, he taught me, to teach his team of executives everything he knew about his business. He realized this process would cause his team to grow. If he ever achieved that goal of teaching them everything he knew, he would no longer be able to serve them, he said. That was his motivation to continue to educate himself.

His philosophy is consistent with an overriding theme of this book, which is finding motivation through serving others. Instead of looking at continuing education as a way to build up his own self-esteem, Don saw it as a way to be effective in serving others. As a result, his business flourished. He developed a loyal following and did so all without ever focusing on building his own self-esteem. I am grateful to Don for his lessons. They continue to serve me well.

Legacy achievers follow this same philosophy when it comes to continuing education. We must learn more if we are going to become more effective at our chosen career or vocation. Additional knowledge is a great motivator.

No matter what we do, we can always improve. Improvement is achieved through increasing knowledge and appropriately applying it. Education plays an important role in balance because every balance point is affected by knowledge. We can't eat right if we don't know what eating right means. We can't invest properly if we don't know how to invest. We can't have faith if we don't know what to put our faith in. We can't share with our family if we don't know what our family holds dear. And we can't help our neighbor if we don't know he's in need.

As you noticed, this section is subtitled, *Knowledge in Motion*. This is because knowledge rarely leads to prosperity if it's kept in a static state in our minds. Thousands of people have enough knowledge to be motivated and therefore successful, but lack a portion of the formula for motivation. As a result, their knowledge is out of proportion to their achievements.

These people are like a Ferrari motor inside a Pacer body. Because they lack part of the formula, they are not able to take full advantage of the motor underneath the hood. The reverse scenario also exists in the world. Some people have every component of the formula for motivation in the palm of their hand, but lack the knowledge it takes to make the formula effective. These people are Ferrari bodies powered by Pacer engines. They can easily handle the turns ahead but lack the power to race forward.

It's important to continue educating ourselves, for in no other way can we harness the full power of the formula for enhancing our life.

Faith ~

It takes a lot more faith to live this life
without faith than with it.

—— Peter DeVries

The history of the United States of America is one of the greatest case studies demonstrating what faith can do for us here on earth. This wonderful and powerful country was undeniably founded upon the beliefs of men and women with strong faith. Proof of this is everywhere.

The Declaration of Independence gives God credit for all things and clearly states that we have a Creator who gave us unalienable rights such as life, liberty and the pursuit of happiness.

Our paper money and coins bear the legend, IN GOD WE TRUST.

Our founding fathers based the legal system on the Ten Commandments.

Even mid 20th century leaders of our great nation acknowledged God. In 1952, an act of Congress changed the Pledge of Allegiance to include the wording "under God."

Yet today our society has developed an attitude that we should no longer talk openly about God because we might offend some of those around us.

We are all affected by this attitude. As a businessperson I am limited to what I can say in reference to God when

> ... leaving out faith and spirituality as a reason for success is like leaving out the bread when making a sandwich. It's what holds everything together.

working with corporations. With an eye for the necessity of being politically correct, I am careful not to cross the line when I work with companies.

However, as a motivational speaker and trainer, I have a problem: leaving out faith and spirituality as a reason for success is like leaving out the bread when making a sandwich. It's what holds everything together.

It's ironic that every dollar businesses receive bears the words, IN GOD WE TRUST, yet it's politically incorrect to mention Him out loud. Who are we trying to protect?

There are only two possibilities when it comes to our human existence. Either we came into existence through random events statistically exceeding what knowledgeable human beings regard as being scientifically probable, or we were created by God. There are no other options. As responsible human beings, we should each examine the possibility of God's existence.

If we determine there is more evidence to support the existence of God than His nonexistence, we should find out what His expectations are for us. Gallup polls have determined that 96% of American's believe in God. If we believe God exists, then we probably believe in the possibility of life after death. What kind of an effect does such a belief have on our lives here on earth?

Legacy achievers take their responsibility to seek out the truth very seriously. A failure to do so can leave a feeling of emptiness.

I believe in God. Too much proof exists to deny His existence. I believe He reveals Himself in many ways. The more I study scripture and history, the more I see that He has a plan for each of us. The more I pray, the more I understand His plan for me.

Understanding His plan for each of us means we need to spin each plate every day. Some of the plates may just need a tiny nudge, but they all need our attention. Perhaps all the attention we can give on a given day is merely thinking about the next time we will be able to pay greater attention to that particular balance point. But always remember, on the days we are unable to actually invest into a new stock, call our mother, serve our neighbor, learn more about our vocation, or find a treadmill to exercise on, there is always time for prayer. God planned it this way.

Summing up Balance

More material on each of the balance points in life is available than we have time to read. Magazine articles, books, sites on the Internet, and other resources are right at our fingertips. However, we already possess the most important thing needed to start balancing our life. This vital starting resource is awareness that we must focus on the six balance points of faith, family, finances, health, education/vocation, and social contribution. This awareness can make an everlasting impact on your life.

As a businessperson, I am constantly reminded of the importance of awareness. I often give important statistics to the people I work with, statistics necessary for the business to operate effectively. Many times, without training or motivating the team, I see sales numbers and other vital business measurements improve by as much as 100% just by making known what the target is. Awareness is essential to improvement and balance.

Simply being aware of the balance points will not equal change in our lives unless we set our awareness in motion. There is no greater time like the present to put balance into our lives.

Defining Concepts

Let's further examine the Balance component of the formula for motivation. We refer to balance in the formula as "The Pursuit of Life's Perfect Balance." Perhaps this sounds intimidating. Sometimes words with great magnitude, such as *perfect*, or words lacking finality such as *pursuit*, tend to make us want to give up before we start.

Relax. As soon as you gain a full understanding of the concepts involved, you'll be anxious to accept the challenge.

Pursuing? Perfect?

I don't claim to be perfect. Far from it. That's why it's necessary to define the concept of *pursuing life's perfect balance* word-for-word. This section focuses on my definition of the words *pursuing* and *perfect*.

I use the word *pursuing* rather than *achieving* because *achieving* suggests that people can finish a job and then rest on their laurels. But pursuing balance and maintaining motivation require lifetime effort.

All words are symbols for the meanings they convey. However, the way I use the word *perfect*—whether as an adjective, noun, or verb— carries the symbolism to a higher level. This is because no human can ever actually *perfect* anything, including balance. However perfection is a necessary target. We use perfection as our target because it requires continued effort. If we shoot for an abstract goal like "pretty good," we have difficulty defining it and may feel as though we have already reached it. Thus we may find ourselves floundering in life without a clear direction or purpose.

Picture a surfer. You see him or her on a surfboard gliding along a huge wave, and say to yourself, "Wow, that guy is incredible! What perfect balance."

Just as you say, "What perfect balance," the surfer slips off balance a bit, and then gets back on balance, then slips off again, then on again. Although, technically, he never actually attains perfect balance, you call it *perfect balance*, because the surfer never falls. It's more accurate to say he *pursues perfect* balance by leaning in different directions.

It's impossible for him to attain perfect balance because the ocean, except for tides and currents, moves in unpredictable ways. Likewise, sometimes we lean a little left. We lean a little right. But if we don't fall off our surfboard in life, we are in the same state of perfect balance as the surfer. Just as the ocean is unpredictable, so are the events in our lives. The more the surfer practices balance, the better prepared he is for the unexpected. With a high level of motivation, our chances for success are great. But we must work on maintaining our balance in life all the time.

> Just as the ocean is unpredictable, so are the events in our lives.

Pursuing Perfection vs. Being a Perfectionist

Let's look at the difference between pursuing *perfection* in balance and being a *perfectionist*. Where is the focus of the perfectionist? On insignificant things, often throughout their entire day. Perfectionists often miss deadlines, because small details delay the real point of the projects in progress. In the grand scheme of things, some tiny details are hardly significant. As opposed to the perfectionist, the person pursuing perfection often has a thorough understanding of the old saying, *The devil is in the details*. That person also pays attention to the big picture and to the significant things in life.

It may appear either noble or naïve to pursue perfect balance, knowing it can never actually be achieved. But in this instance, consider the pursuit noble, knowing that you're reaching for the truly big picture in life.

Be Not Afraid

Someone said, "Why don't you call your work on the formula for motivation *The Pursuit of Great Balance* or *The Pursuit of Really Good Balance*? Perfection sounds so difficult!"

This is true. But as I talked with legacy achievers I found that they don't pursue great balance or really good balance in life. To them, those adjectives just aren't measurable, they're much too flexible. Define great? Define really good? These definitions are much too relative for this purpose.

Perfection is measurable

By definition a square is only a square if it's perfect. But we still call our imperfect attempts at drawing them, squares. That being said, perfection is measurable very much in the same way you teach a young child to copy a square.

You don't just give the child a great square or a good square to copy because it wouldn't really be a square. You give the child a *perfect* square, because if the child actually duplicates a great or good square exactly, it won't be a square because a square must be perfect. So, the target must be perfection.

Give a three-year-old a square and ask the child to duplicate it. We know she is not going to get it exactly right. The child makes something resembling a square. If you're the child's parent or teacher, you're not going to get on her case for not making a perfect square at age three. You say, "Hey. Good job! Keep working on it." With that, the pursuit of perfection begins.

Although the child may not be capable of drawing a perfect square freehanded you would still encourage her to do so. The following year, when you give her the same square to duplicate, you expect the child to do little better. If she doesn't draw a better square, you work with her until the square is better. It's about improvement.

Pursuing perfect balance is a process we go through continuously. Every year as the child gets older, he or she gets closer to that perfect square. Ultimately, with the appropriate tools, the child draws a perfect square and you say, "Now that's perfect."

Likewise, we all need to develop our focus on perfect balance. We also need to be forgiving of ourselves and forgiving of others when we fall short of our objective.

To pursue something as special as perfect balance, we need to realize we are going to make mistakes. If we get down or feel low because we don't attain perfect balance, or don't feel in balance one day, we might want to give up on the whole concept. Some of us would concede, "I just can't do it."

This is where forgiveness comes in. Nobody ever attains *perfection*. That goal is always a work in progress. We develop our focus on perfect balance throughout life.

It's wise to go through the process saying, "I know nobody actually *attains* perfection. The objective is to get as close as I can."

Consider people who think they are perfect or say they've attained perfect balance. The admission itself exposes the flaw. Even legacy achievers don't identify themselves as such. When you're in balance, ultimately the square you copy may not be perfect but you will have found motivation in your continued pursuit.

The mistakes that we make during our pursuit help form our character and lead us closer to that ever-evasive goal of perfection. Our flaws and imperfections shape us into something that can ultimately become beautiful.

It's like a flower. When you look at a flower, you may say, "This flower is beautiful, how perfect!" But look closer. You'll see flaws and imperfections. But in the right arrangement, those flaws and imperfections make up a "perfect" flower.

Focus on the Destination

For another way to look at pursuing perfection look at how a pilot and co-pilot fly a jetliner.

Jet planes fly slightly off-course about ninety to ninety-five percent of the time. Today, an auto-pilot constantly corrects these deviations, but before this feature came into use, the pilot and co-pilot handled the errors. They didn't sit in the cockpit saying, "C'mon. What are you doing?" They didn't smack each other on the head and say, "Hey, you're off course by a degree. Keep this up and we'll wind up in San Diego instead of Los Angeles."

The pilots' primary focus was on where they were scheduled to go. They didn't pay much attention to being slightly off course at any given moment. As a matter of fact, they didn't even look at the situation as a mistake; they simply made the necessary correction, and considered it part of the process.

So look at the flaws in your journey toward perfect balance the same way pilots view course corrections made during flight—they are simply part of the process. When you feel your destination is right in front of you, don't get egotistical, thinking you've reached perfection. This is when real trouble may strike. Life may throw us a curve and we may need to rebalance to get back on course again.

A Big Lesson from a Little Bit

An American company developed a drill bit as thin as a human hair. This was considered an amazing technological feat at the time. The development occurred during the collapse of the former Russian Empire.

The company introduced its amazing drill bit all over the world, and sent samples to Germany, Russia, and Japan.

The Russians didn't respond, no doubt due to the fall of communism, starving people, and other more pressing matters.

The Germans were extremely interested. Their response: Send all the information you can. How did you develop this? What are the applications? How could this bit be used in our marketplace?

The Japanese simply mailed the drill bit back _with a hole drilled through it_!

The point is, no matter how great or perfect we might think we are, there is always room for improvement. We might

> People who stretch themselves to grow, train for upcoming and unexpected challenges, making themselves fit for life's coming adventures.

say to ourselves "I don't want to put the effort into improving my life. It's fine just the way it is."

But for how long? Without a focus on improvement, we are only capable of handling the same types of challenges that life has already given us. People who stretch themselves to grow, train for upcoming and unexpected challenges, making themselves fit for life's coming adventures.

Conversely people who have a *my-life-is-fine-just-the-way-it-is* attitude, often are forced to grow in the midst of turmoil. Unfortunately being forced to grow can be more painful than choosing to grow.

Inspiring Examples

Authors Jack Canfield and Mark Victor Hansen put together a compilation of well-known people who have overcome difficulties to accomplish great things. Examples such as these should be an inspiration for us in the pursuit of life's perfect balance. The authors described how:

> After Fred Astaire's first screen test, MGM's testing director wrote, "Can't act, slightly bald, can dance a little."

> When Astaire became one of Hollywood's greatest stars, he had this memo framed and hung over the fireplace in his palatial Beverly Hills home.

An expert said of the renowned coach Vince Lombardi, "He possesses minimal football knowledge and lacks motivation."

Can you believe how far wrong the *expert's* assessment was? Today, Vince Lombardi is famous as one of the greatest motivators of modern times, and he owns one of the greatest records any coach ever achieved in the National Football League.

Louisa May Alcott, author of the classic *Little Women*, was encouraged to find work as a servant or seamstress by her family.

Beethoven handled the violin awkwardly and preferred playing his own compositions to improving his violin technique. His teachers considered him hopeless as a composer.

The parents of the famous opera singer, Enrico Caruso, wanted him to be an engineer. His teacher said he had no voice and could not sing.

Walt Disney was fired by a newspaper editor for lack of ideas.

Thomas Edison's teacher said he was too stupid to learn anything.

Albert Einstein did not speak until he was four years old and did not read until he was seven. His teachers described him as mentally slow, unsociable, and adrift forever in his foolish dreams. He was refused admittance to the Zurich Polytechnic School.

Henry Ford went broke five times before he finally succeeded.

Babe Ruth, considered by many sports historians to be the greatest athlete of all time, is famous for setting a home run record that wasn't approached for many years. Ruth also held the record for strikeouts.

Winston Churchill failed sixth grade. He did not become England's Prime Minister until he was sixty-two years old. His late success came after a lifetime of defeats and setbacks. Churchill made his greatest contributions as a senior citizen.

Eighteen publishers turned down Richard Bock's ten-thousand-word story, *Jonathan Livingstone Seagull*, before McMillan published it in 1970. By 1975, the book had sold more than seven million copies in the US alone.

When we find ourselves feeling discouraged, it helps to know that others have felt the same way but did not give up. Their focus allowed them to continue to pursue greatness in their lives. The same can hold true for us.

The pursuit of perfection is a lifetime pursuit which includes failures and often harsh criticism from others. We must be wise enough to forgive our own mistakes as well as strong enough to stay on track when we are fairly or unfairly judged by others.

My dad's advice for me as a young man about to begin my first job was to listen to my critics, because he said I would often learn more from them than I would those who gave me praise.

Beginning the process of living a highly motivated and balanced life is certainly not out of anyone's reach. But to do so you must focus on the reasons why you want to balance your life, never on the excuses for why you can't.

People who strive for perfection become more aware of the work they must accomplish in life because they have a lofty and specific target. People who have no specific target can stagnate in life.

In a speech to Parliament on June 8, 1944, Prime Minister Winston Churchill said, "I'm sure the mistakes of the time (referring to World War I) will not be repeated. We shall probably make a whole new set of mistakes." Churchill's statement describes human nature. Of course, his prediction came true.

Forgiving ourselves for our mistakes should not be confused with compromising our standards. We must not become complacent and accept our mistakes because we feel they are inevitable. That attitude would, in a way, constitute quitting before starting.

Abraham Esra said, "A little sin is big when a big man commits it."

Simply put, we must always hold ourselves to a higher standard. We must discern the difference between forgiving ourselves for our mistakes and simply accepting them.

What Is Your Role in Life?

In order to help provide meaning to our pursuit of life's perfect balance, we must discover what our role is in this world. To do this we must examine our God-given talents and gifts to explore what that role may be.

Here's a thought I've often had. If we could take *The Guinness Book of World Records* and ask every single person on earth to try and break every record in the book, I believe it would only be a matter of days before we would have to rewrite most of the records.

Think about our planet's six billion inhabitants. Among this vast number of people, how many individuals who have never put on track shoes could be faster than the greatest world-class sprinters?

How many people who have never put on boxing gloves could get in the ring with Evander Holyfield, Mike Tyson, or Lennox Lewis and defeat them?

How many people could write beautiful poetry but never picked up a pen for that purpose?

How many people have the natural talent to play musical instruments but have never tried to develop the talent?

Contemplating your direction in life can be exciting to think about. We all need to find our talents and our purpose. The pursuit of perfection guides us toward this discovery.

Roger Banister used one of his gifts very well. On May 6, 1954, Banister ran the first ever sub-four-minute mile. He ran the mile in three minutes, fifty-nine seconds, thus ending the athletic world's long-running quest to break the four-minute mile.

Today, high school students run sub-four-minute miles regularly and not because Nike· came out with a better shoe. It's because the belief systems of high school students now allow them to accomplish the same feat.

Rogers' role in life goes well beyond breaking a track record. His dramatic accomplishment shapes the minds of many people who face today's challenges. His story serves as one of the most common inspirational stories used by coaches and business leaders everyday.

It's doubtful whether Banister had the slightest inkling of the enormous impact his story would still be having on the world of athletics and business decades after the event. So you too may not be aware of the effect your results and achievements may have on others.

Take It To The Next Level

On a much more serious note, I once had the pleasure of meeting US Airforce Colonel Edward L. Hubbard, (Retired). His story really impressed me.

Colonel Hubbard talked about how he was ordered to get up before dawn one day to fly a mission over enemy territory.

He said, "You always know it's going to be a bad day when it's still dark when you get up."

During a speech, he asked his audience, "How many of you have had a bad day before?" Everyone raised a hand.

"Let me see if I can put a bad day into perspective," he continued.

As he was flying over enemy territory, Hubbard's plane was hit. He ejected from his aircraft while it was flying at about six hundred miles an hour. Hubbard described what it was like to hit the air at six hundred miles an hour. He said it was like hitting a brick wall. The impact was so great, he was blinded when he hit the air.

The colonel fell through the dark sky, blind and painfully aware he was being shot at from the ground. He did what anyone would do. He reached up to feel his face to learn the extent of the injury and realized he wasn't blind. His helmet had just spun around on his head and covered his face.

When he turned the helmet around he saw a sight as terrifying as falling blind. He could see the enemy fire coming at him. But he landed without being hit, was immediately captured, and spent many years as a prisoner of war.

Some things he accomplished to keep himself alive in prison were absolutely amazing. Colonel Hubbard knew that to survive in prison he needed to keep physically and mentally sharp.

His physical survival was assisted by a Navy friend just a couple of cells away. The Navy man challenged him to a push-up contest. He communicated to Hubbard, "Let's see how many we can do."

Hubbard took up the challenge. He got down on the floor and performed 100 push-ups. But his Navy friend did 150 and said, "I win."

Hubbard replied, "Okay, let's do it again. Only next time, you go first."

Hubbard figured this time he'd know what his competition was, and then he could beat him.

After a few weeks of preparation the contest commenced. The Navy friend powered 200 push-ups.

So Hubbard followed with 220 push-ups, winning the contest. For the next encounter, the Naval pilot asked the Colonel to go first. They repeated the whole process. This time, Colonel Hubbard performed 300 consecutive push-ups.

His Navy friend did 600 push-ups in a row.

Wisely, Colonel Hubbard said, "I don't want to do this contest anymore. Let's do sit-ups."

So, they had a sit-ups contest, and the Colonel's friend completed 2,000 sit-ups in row. Now, Colonel Hubbard had never done more than 115 sit-ups, the number required for his Air Force officer fitness test. But, he ended up doing 2,700 consecutive sit-ups to win the contest.

Keep in mind these feats were accomplished on a prison diet that was often as low as 300 calories a day. A normal diet would provide about 2,000 calories.

Sometimes when you think you're tapped out physically, and don't have enough energy to accomplish what you must accomplish, remember, you can—as these men did—take it to the next level.

You are capable of taking all your quests to levels you can't seriously believe you can reach at this moment.

Mind Games

To maintain mental sharpness during years of captivity, Colonel Hubbard conducted mental feats as impressive as his physical achievements.

He accomplished these amazing mental acts in the stressful setting of a prison camp, while witnessing other patriots being beaten by guards. Prisoners were not allowed to speak to each other. Talking meant a beating or even death.

One way the prisoners communicated was with tap code, a method the military taught.

Picture a square grid containing 25 boxes. Five boxes across, five boxes down. Each box contains a letter of the alphabet starting with A in the upper left corner (The letter "k" was eliminated because "c" could be substituted for it.).

To communicate using tap code, tap the number of boxes a letter is across and down. For example, tap three times for the letter C–the third box to the right in the top row.

Imagine tapping out just one word. To speed the tedious process a little, the prisoners developed codes for certain words. But to communicate they still had to tap everything—but one thing they had plenty of was time.

Colonel Hubbard and other prisoners who wanted to stay mentally fit were determined to keep on learning while in prison. Just imagine the psychological difficulties coming from sitting in a prison camp for years, unable to even speak to another person.

So they tapped to each other and asked, "What do you know that I don't know? What do I know that you don't know?"

"Let's share all we know." Tap. Tap. Tap.

One man spoke Spanish. So, Colonel Hubbard decided to learn Spanish in tap code. He excelled in the language. Tap. Tap. Tap.

When released years later, the Colonel visited a university near his home and asked the Spanish professor if he could take the final exam. Hubbard passed the final although he had never heard the language spoken before he took the test.

I recommend his book *Escape from the Box: The Wonder of Human Potential*. I am grateful to Colonel Hubbard for teaching me more about expanding my mind and my body to reach another level in my pursuit of perfect life balance.

We can all use these stories of courage and triumph as a source of strength if we feel ourselves losing balance or motivation.

Pursuing life's perfect balance is about incremental improvement. The pursuit is about forgiveness. We need to forgive our own mistakes along the way because mistakes are part of the process. We must focus on making fewer and fewer mistakes on our journey. We must focus on becoming a more effective person as time goes on.

~ ~ ~

Part Two

Tactical Components

*"Try not to become a man of success but rather
try to become a man of value."*

—— Albert Einstein

Chapter 3

Integrity Based Influence (IBI)

Reflecting on many years spent researching influence, the primary thing ringing in my head is the importance of integrity. Numerous books have been written on influence, most of them based on a disappointing popular philosophy about influence. This philosophy essentially teaches people to do, say, or act in any way possible to advance their cause, with little or no mention of the importance of integrity.

Readers are told they'll find techniques in these books to convince people to do what they want, without considering anyone's feelings, well being, or rights except their own. Not surprisingly, since the authors urge disregard for the legitimate needs of others, few of the techniques can deliver on the book's promises. However, this is beside the point.

Due to my own immaturity I found some techniques that worked early in my career, and I used them. I regret doing so. That being said, the lessons learned from my mistakes are now invaluable. Now I can see the greater problem: in those days I could always justify my actions. My conscience was in constant turmoil but my results as a businessperson were incredible. Sales boomed.

When confronted by my conscience, I rationalized that I was simply implementing what I learned from my studies. Besides, I wasn't doing anything that the general population would have considered wrong. In fact, most people would have considered using the techniques prudent. As a result, I became and remained a master of technique until I could no longer handle the pain in my heart.

> Could I still get solid sales results if I abandoned the self-centered techniques that worked so well?

A new challenge faced me. Could I still get solid sales results if I abandoned the self-centered techniques that worked so well? Could I follow my conscience and still be successful? I was in a crisis. I could not continue as I was. My motivation was deteriorating because I was not being true to my conscience.

I took a leap of faith and began to monitor everything I said from the perspective of the other person. After, what I considered a brief correctional period, my results where even greater than they had been before.

Focusing on the other person did not mean excluding all of the information and techniques I'd been taught about influence. Although most of that information lacked integrity, not all of it did. Not using anything I had learned would be throwing the baby out with the bath water. The difference was that I not only incorporated integrity into how I influenced others, I put it first.

I am thankful that I learned this lesson prior to assuming a substantial leadership role. Learning the same lesson while having a lot of people reporting to me would have caused me deeper regret.

The negative effects of *technique driven influence tactics* can be seen most clearly in sales management. Sales managers often teach their salespeople a technique called a "tie down." An example of a tie down would be looking at someone and nodding your head up and down in the yes motion as you deliver a loaded question such as "So you *would* like to buy it, right?" Admittedly, this is a natural unconscious tendency but when it is done to consciously manipulate others, it lacks integrity.

The objective is to get the customer so wrapped up in your body language and voice inflection that they essentially forget their own opinion and do as you say.

As if this isn't bad enough, sales managers often use the same technique directly on the salespeople they're managing. They will look directly at the sales reps with their head nodding vigorously up and down and say, "So *you will* get the samples ready for me by 9:00, *right?*"

If the reps are using their brains, they know they were just manipulated in the same disrespectful manner in which they were taught to treat their own customers.

Here's the good news: many people in the world are influential without being manipulative.

The objective of this chapter is to share with you how influence fits into the life of a legacy achiever. As I mentioned earlier, my motivation to continue to work hard was deteriorating because I was not following my conscience. I was using influence tactically, but without integrity. While today's society wouldn't call anything I ever did unethical, I knew in my heart that something wasn't right. One's ethics

> One's ethics should not be measured by the deteriorated state of society, but by the standard of right and wrong.

should not be measured by the deteriorated state of society, but by the standard of right and wrong.

In business we are often faced with ethical decisions. An attorney advised me how to keep a foreign businessperson in the country after her work visa expired. He explained how to fill out the paperwork to satisfy the government.

"We'll never have to honor the letter as long as the government doesn't find out," the attorney added.

"That would lack integrity," I said.

"People do this all the time," he responded.

Unfortunately this attitude is all too common today. The attorney was using the absence of other people's integrity or society's deteriorated state to justify his own lack of integrity. Of course we honored the terms of the letter.

By Itself, Influence Is Not Enough

Rather than placing our focus on influence alone, I urge *integrity based influence* (IBI) as the most powerful tactical component of motivation.

IBI is necessary when it comes to living a motivated life for many reasons. Time and time again, I meet with people who are unhappy in their jobs because their employers ask them to take actions that are against their ethics or morals. For example, salespeople are often trained to provide false information just to secure a sale. Middle managers are told to lie to employees in order to cover up unethical practices of their superiors.

Trainers or managers who lack integrity teach their salespeople to do the same—without admitting what they are doing. Rather, they call their unprincipled advice a *sales technique* and persist with this disguise even though everyone knows what they are doing.

When top executives ask a middle manager to lie, they usually buddy up to the manager with an opportunity talk about the future. Or they let the manager in on a secret so he feels important. This way the manager has greater incentive to lie.

When managers are pressured to lie to, or manipulate others, a decision must be made. Usually they have only two options: lower their moral standards in order to fit in, or quit. This major cause of employee turnover in corporations is especially damaging to the firms involved because it usually drives their best and brightest managers away.

Sometimes there's a third option—which often turns out to be only a temporary solution. They can refuse to lie, and hang on in hopes the corporate culture will change in time to save their jobs. It rarely happens soon enough, and to hang on they have to accept diminished prospects or even open hostility from management. If they elect to stay, no matter which option the pressed-to-lie manager chooses, his or her motivation deteriorates.

Being asked to compromise our integrity can be detrimental, but choosing to do so on our own is even more destructive. If we do this, we will lose our perpetual motivation because we either suffer from a guilty conscience or eventually are exposed as untrustworthy.

Exercising our influence can help us guard our time and emotions against outside factors that are inconsistent with living in balance. In life we are constantly pulled in many directions. If we lack the ability to effectively influence others, we can lose control of our lives. This is why we must learn Integrity Based Influence. If we utilize integrity the way it is described in IBI, we are well on our way to experiencing perpetual motivation.

The Seven Identifiable Traits of IBI People

There are seven identifiable traits consistently present in the behavior of people who use IBI, many of whom become legacy achievers. These traits are *not* techniques. In other words, we are not going to focus on what legacy achievers *do* to people in order to influence them. Instead we'll zero in on the characteristics from which legacy achievers derive their power to influence others.

Trait #1: Keep Your Emotions on a Leash

Although I rarely watch daytime television talk shows, curiosity got the best of me when I passed by a television while leaving the gym one day. I saw a woman relate a traumatic experience she'd had on a Sunday. The lady concluded with, "Sundays are my depression days," thus dooming herself to being unhappy 1/7th of the rest of her life.

A traumatic event can anchor itself to certain circumstances, in this case Sundays, and cause us to recall unwanted emotions when similar circumstances arise—this much is understandable. Nevertheless, if we want to live a

Legacy achievers keep their emotions on a leash.

motivated life, we must learn to control our emotions.

Before we can influence others in positive ways, we need to be able to influence ourselves positively. If we allow ourselves to perpetuate the emotions generated by the negative events of our life, we condemn ourselves to fighting a never-ending battle with self-inflicted de-motivation.

The talk show guest, behaving irrationally, transferred an extreme aversion to a day of the week. Even though most people behave far more rationally, many endlessly dwell on past mistakes and unfortunate experiences. It's a habit, and like all habits, it can be broken.

It's difficult to influence others if we can't control our own emotions because we appear weak or unstable. In addition, our uncontrolled emotions can cloud our ability to make good decisions.

When our emotions flare up, identifying where they came from and what they are trying to make us do is vital. For example, consider the natural defense mechanism called *fight or flight*. This instinct, triggered by fear, is built into every human being. If we are in a life-threatening situation and fail to convert our fear into action, we will probably die. Generally the source of the fear is obvious, but if not, we must identify it. Then we must make a decision to either separate ourselves from the danger, or face and fight it.

Typically, these situations involve fear, depression, guilt, anxiety or some other negative emotion. Our first step in dealing with this kind of situation should be to analyze where the fear generating the situation comes from, and decide whether we can and should gather more information before choosing flight or fight.

Sometimes there'll be no time for such niceties, but if the situation is a recurring one, we will certainly have ample time to study our best course of action. However, a decision such as submitting to making Sundays an automatic day of depression is tantamount to being immobilized with fear in the face of death instead of fleeing or fighting.

As long as a person does not suffer from a physiological problem, it's safe to say they could do what many legacy achievers do in this type of situation. Legacy achievers keep their emotions on a leash. They control their emotions rather than letting their emotions control them. In other words, they don't let their emotions run free. Emotions can be like a dog that chases a car until it sees a bus, then chases the bus until it sees a bike, and so on until eventually the dog can't find its way back home. We must allow ourselves to express our emotions in appropriate ways, but never to become lost in them.

Whenever possible legacy achievers preplan emotional strategies. If a legacy achiever is in the sales profession and is aware of the daily and unavoidable objections to be faced, she wisely considers an appropriate emotional response to these rejections. One legacy achiever I know has a sixty-second rule. He allows himself sixty seconds to gain control of his emotions when things don't go well selling. This strategy turns mastering his emotions into a game. In his mind he scores a point for every second, short of a minute, that he can overcome his emotions.

It is strategic to contemplate, though not to dwell on, inevitable situations that will stir our own emotions. When facing an unpleasant inevitability, people often say, "I don't even want to think about it!" Such avoidance can only keep us unprepared emotionally. Contemplating and preplanning emotional reactions can help us deal with situations when they arise.

This does not mean contemplating and preparing for all the potential tragedies in life. Experiencing the emotional

trauma of what it would be like to lose all our family members in a sudden accident is not an accurate interpretation of the point. On the other hand, if a close friend or relative has a terminal condition, it's wise to prepare yourself.

On a less serious but still very stressful topic, if your company is downsizing and you know you may be next, don't ignore the probability. Face it. Prepare yourself to accept the situation if you become a casualty of the change. Your preparation should include developing a plan to move past the misfortune.

When all is said and done legacy achievers handle their emotions in a similar way to what is asked for in the Serenity Prayer:

> God grant me the serenity to accept the things
> I can not change, the courage to change the things I
> can, *and the wisdom to know the difference.*

Trait #2: Use Harmony and Conviction in Verbal Communication

"Mean what you say and say what you mean" gives a cliché summary of this second trait. Legacy achievers accomplish this by speaking in harmony with what they stand for and they do so with conviction.

A study published by Dr. Albert Meridian at Berkley, shows that verbal communication contains three components. These components are, the *word choices* we make, the *voice qualities* we use and our *physiology*.

His study found that the *words* we use represent only 7% of our influence. Our *voice quality*—made up of our tone, tempo, and volume—represents 38% of our influence. Finally our *physiology*, or body language, makes up the balance and majority of our influence by accounting for 55% of it.

This information could very easily lead a person down the wrong path of influence. Non-integrity based influential people choose to amplify their manipulative skills by practicing techniques that make effective use of Dr. Meridian's findings. I've seen this happen. It results in transparent communicators limited to influencing only people who are weaker than themselves.

Instead, an IBI person or legacy achiever uses this information to determine if he or she may be accidentally sending the wrong messages by presenting unintentional inconsistencies in his or her delivery. This is not a painless thing to do. It may require us to recognize a fault of which we are presently unaware. With the permission of everyone involved, video taping or audio taping some of the conversations we have is an excellent way to identify inconsistencies so we can eliminate them.

I often have my own speeches video taped in order to see what message the audience received in comparison to the message I intended to deliver. Occasionally it can be a very humbling experience to be in your own audience but it's wise to use today's technology to make us aware of our current skill level, whatever it might be.

The importance of harmony in our verbal communication skills is illustrated by what happens when we lack harmony. We strike harmony in verbal communication by sending the same message with our word choices, voice quality and body language. These must also be in agreement with our convictions. If any one of these are lacking, the perceived result can range from humor to sarcasm or even rudeness.

If I said the kind words "You look nice" in a harsh voice with a snarl on my face, what message would you perceive?

You might conclude that I think you look stupid.

You may think I really feel you look nice but I'm too embarrassed to say it in a normal way.

You may think I meant what I said, but it came out funny because I was in the middle of a yawn.

You may think I'm being rude.

In other words, what should have been a simple communication was hopelessly confused. Whatever I really meant probably didn't get through to you.

When we lack congruency in our message we leave the recipient guessing what we meant, which leads to insecurity. This is why legacy achievers are cautious about using sarcasm. People want to know where they stand with one another; sarcasm does not allow for that.

Conviction is very important because it tends to clarify messages that might otherwise be misinterpreted. Conviction eliminates the need for excess words.

You're an employer. One of your employees asks, "Do you have confidence in me as an employee?" You respond by avoiding eye contact and softly saying, "You're a great employee, and I really appreciate you."

What will he think? Probably he'll doubt that you mean what you said. He may go away far more worried than he was before he asked the question.

On the other hand if you look him directly in the eyes and firmly say, "Yes" with a strong nod of conviction, he will rest assured that you meant what you said. One word spoken with conviction can be far more effective than an entire

One word spoken with conviction can be far more effective than an entire speech without it.

speech without it. Of course an IBI person would only say yes if he or she really meant it. In other words, this is not about technique; it's about disclosing your true feelings to the other person.

Trait #3: Anticipate

Henry Nodland was an interesting fellow. He dressed like a lumberjack and drove a Cadillac. During the 1940s he served as the mayor in a small town of Minnesota. One day this self-made millionaire was driving through a neighboring town when he was pulled over for speeding and ticketed for $50.00. Before he drove on, Henry asked the officer if he would be in the same area checking traffic later in the day.

"I will," the policeman said.

"Here's another $50.00," Henry said. "I'll be coming back!"

When people focus on IBI, they develop the art of anticipation. While I might question Henry's approach in this day and age, he certainly does illustrate three rules for effective anticipation. **First**, know where you plan to go. **Second**, be on the lookout for obstacles. **Third**, be willing to pay the price ahead of time.

Legacy achievers keep these three things in mind regarding all the balance points. Now let's focus on how the three rules of anticipation affect influence.

Know where you plan to go

When Henry asked whether or not the police officer was going to be on the street in a few hours, it was because Henry knew he'd be on his way back through town. If Henry hadn't planned his day prior to encountering the man in blue, he wouldn't have known enough to ask the question.

This sounds like a basic concept and it may be in much of your life. We plan strategies for vacations, meals, parties

and more, but what about communication? During verbal communication with others we are often caught off guard and become annoying when we don't have any idea where we're going in our conversation. We may not always have the luxury of preparing our objectives for all our communications but we should be aware of what they are when things really count.

Be on the lookout for obstacles

One day upon arriving home from work my wife, Lisa greeted me with a concern. Our daughter Nicole, who was in kindergarten at the time, was concerned about her older brother Kevin, who attended the same school in the first grade. Nicole told Lisa that some older kids were tackling Kevin this week at recess, and it looked like it might be hurting him. Lisa wanted to wait for me to arrive home before talking too much about the issue with Kevin. I guess she was thinking I may have had a similar playground experience as a boy, and would know whether or not to brush off the concern. She said the only thing she asked Kevin was whether or not he liked the older kids treating him this way. He told her *he did not like it.*

I was not sure what to think. I didn't like the idea of my son being bullied at school but I wasn't sure what to say to him. Being a second-degree black belt, I must admit for a split second, I actually considered giving him a crash course on self-defense. Then I thought, maybe it would build his character to let him deal with it himself. Then I thought, maybe the best solution might be to talk to a teacher or a parent of one of the older kids. I really didn't know what I should do. But I did know I needed more information.

So I asked him,

"Kevin, is there anything you want to tell me about recess today?"

He replied

"No, not really Dad."

Thinking he might just be afraid to speak out against the other kids, I thought I would prompt him.

"Were some older kids tackling you at school today?" In a quick one-word reply, he said, "Yes"

"Are they playing with you or is this something you don't like them doing?"

"I don't like it." He reluctantly said.

It hurt me as a parent to know that my son was being picked on. I, myself, never really faced that at school. I felt sorry for him and realized I needed to give this some thought. But before we ended the conversation I needed to find out one more thing.

"Kevin how old were these boys?"

"Dad, they weren't boys!"

I couldn't believe my ears. They're not boys, "Good grief," I thought, "my son is being bullied by girls! What psychological problems might this be responsible for in the future?" Before I could finish my thought I heard Lisa ask, in a way that only she could have put it,

"Kevin, were these girls lovin' ya up or were they beatin' ya up?"

"Loving me up. I don't want to talk about it!"

Now that was the first thing he said in this whole conversation that really made sense to me!

Although this is just an example of being caught off guard in a silly conversation, it's a good reminder. We will benefit by anticipating as many potential outcomes as possible to the important conversations we have each day.

In the situation with Kevin, I wasn't able to select my most appropriate action because my preconceptions ruled out what had actually happened. Thankfully in this case, my only option was to laugh. But that's not always the case.

Attorneys spend weeks preparing for court by role playing the potential outcomes from cross-examining a witness during a trial. All this, just to prepare for what might be a five-minute conversation. But think of what's at stake: lack of preparation might send an innocent person to prison, or let a guilty person walk free. Most of us do not have to deal with outcomes of that magnitude in our daily conversations, still, we must be prepared if we are going to effectively influence others.

Be prepared to pay the price ahead of time

Henry knew where he wanted to go and he identified an obstacle that could slow him down. Faced with this reality Henry decided to pay the price ahead in order to save time. IBI people are also prepared to pay the price ahead of time. In this case we are talking about the price of ridicule or rejection when it comes to a position or stance we feel we must take.

Here's a reality legacy achievers must be prepared to meet with integrity: occasionally other people will not see eye to eye with them. At one time or another, we have all been in a situation where our position was unpopular. In the face of this dilemma, the pressure to compromise one's beliefs and follow the crowd is strong. If we allow this to happen, we lose our integrity, weaken our ability to influence others, and also lose our ability to maintain a high level of motivation.

Am I urging you to adopt an adamantly closed mind, no compromise, take-no-prisoners approach to all questions?

Definitely not. Intellectual integrity implies—yes, even demands —that we be open to persuasion. We can change our minds for good reason and therefore agree with the crowd—if we are truly persuaded by new information, as distinguished from yielding to pressure to go along or conform. In such a case, we show strength and exercise integrity by changing our position. Only when we act against our true position do we lose our integrity.

Trait #4: Be Consistent

Legacy achievers exhibit consistent behavior, and people who are consistent naturally become more influential.

Think about the people who influence you the most? Do they haphazardly change stances on issues, or are they consistent in their beliefs?

Personally, I find it difficult to build relationships with inconsistent people. I never quite know where they stand on any given issue. I have difficulty trusting them.

Remember back to your days in high school. When a new semester began you thought a laid-back, easy teacher was the greatest. But later in the semester when exam time came around, that laid back teacher poured on serious homework and you may have felt betrayed by his or her inconsistency.

In contrast, you probably didn't like the tough teacher who dished out homework from the start, but eventually you came to expect the homework and just dealt with it. When exam time came, you were probably prepared due to the consistency.

In the end, you learned more from and respected the tough teacher. That teacher's potential influence over you far surpassed the other's.

Consistency is a building block for long-term relationships because security and consistency are interwoven

During a discussion on the benefits of consistency, a woman rejected the idea.

"If I'm consistent, I can't act spontaneously. And that's how I live my life," she said. "I'm spontaneous. That's who I am."

"Are you spontaneous all the time?" I asked.

"Yes."

"Well then," I said. "You're consistently spontaneous."

> Consistency is a building block for long-term relationships because security and consistency are interwoven.

Although my response may have sounded flippant, her example illustrates a point about consistency. When around someone who always acts spontaneously, you know you have to be alert, stay on your toes, and be ready for quick changes. In her presence you can find a certain security in knowing that something exciting could happen at any moment. Not everyone can appreciate such a person, but if you can, such people are usually quite fun to have as friends.

Trait #5: Maintain a Healthy Outlook on Competition

Influential people have a tremendous understanding of their own competitive nature. We all inherently possess the desire to compete, even if only in some small way. Either we desire to compete with ourselves or with others around us. Having the desire to compete does not always mean that we choose to compete. Knowing the right time, place, and reason to compete is essential to motivation.

The desire to compete is fueled both positively and negatively. Positive driving forces are things like enjoying a challenge or wanting to improve. Negative driving forces are related to envy, greed, jealousy, power and runaway self-esteem.

Personal competition exists on two levels—internal and external.

Internal competition is the contest between our current selves and our past performances. That internal competition propels us to outperform our own past in order to grow.

External competition is with other people, for most of us this means the people immediately around us.

There are three types of competitive people: passive, selective, and addicted.

Passive Competitors

Some passive competitors deny the existence of a competitive spirit in themselves, which really defies human nature. All people possess some sense of competition. Passively competitive people can accurately say they have great control over their competitive impulses, but to deny their existence is wrong. Legacy achievers or Integrity-Based Influencers control their competitive impulses better than most people can.

Many passive competitors falsely claim they are not competitive because they don't want to put forth the necessary effort to achieve what they desire. Others claim to be noncompetitive because they fear failure.

Envy often drives these attitudes. Someone we'll call Bob claimed he doesn't want a luxury car, yet he always knows who owns one in his circle of acquaintances. Bob makes a

lot of sarcastic remarks about such people, saying things like, "They can't get attention any other way," and "No matter what wheels he has, he's still a fat chrome-dome."

It's a safe bet that Bob secretly lusts for a BMW of his own but knows he can't afford one. Instead of knuckling down to earn one, he uses denial and attack as defense mechanisms.

On the other hand, legacy achievers who claim not to desire a luxury car have no interest in who drives what. At least two multi-billionaires, the Reform Party's Ross Perot, and Amazon.com's founder, Jeff Bezos, drive themselves around in modest cars. Do you think they know or care whether there's a Rolls-Royce in every garage on their street except theirs?

Truly passive competitors can become very influential because their integrity and low-key approach make them like E.F. Hutton, "When they talk, people listen."

Addicted Competitors

The addicted competitor goes over board on competition and has a difficult time controlling his or her desire to compete, even in trivial matters. Some addicted competitors seem to have a mechanism in their mind connecting the ability to win directly to their self-esteem. For this type of addicted competitor, the spirit of competition is not as important as winning is. Other addicted competitors just can't stand the idea of someone having something they don't, even if that something is simply the satisfaction of winning.

A great example of an addicted competitor is the guy who pulls up next to you at a red light and takes off like a drag racer when the light turns green. The addicted competitor must get in front of you even if he or she is not in a hurry. You'll often catch up with him a few blocks later and he's barely going the speed limit. The drag racer just had to be in the lead. He just *had to compete.*

Another example is the guy who gets angry over losing a card game with friends. He makes the others uncomfortable and loses their respect. Addicted competitors generally do not become legacy achievers because they lack influence. Most people who get to know these people have a hard time taking them seriously because they treat *every*thing as a competition and are always in high gear. They are often seen as one-dimensional, even if they are not. We have all run into this type of person, at one time or another. Some of us, including myself, may occasionally act like this person to a certain degree. But when we find ourselves all wrapped up in a pointless competition yet having a hard time resolving it, we must view our actions as others do, (pretty stupid) and get over it!

Selective Competitors

The selective competitor calculates when it is appropriate to compete. He or she carefully determines what drives their competitive spirit. Being a selective competitor makes a legacy achiever influential because they are seen as reasonable to the general public. Selective competitors are not only people that know when to compete, but they also have an impressive winning record.

Selective competitors are winners because they take time to determine what is important to them and focus on developing the skills to accomplish it. This does not mean that they completely avoid things that they do poorly. It simply means that they put those things in perspective when they participate in them.

For example, a selective competitor goes skiing with better skiers than herself, but she would not jump a cliff to prove that she is the best.

Selective competitors compete wisely. Unlike addicted competitors who try to force their way to victories, selective competitors use strategy and finesse.

An addicted competitor racing an Indy car finds it difficult to let other drivers pass him when stopping at the pit to fuel up and get a change of tires. The selective competitor sees the long-term value of the pit stop despite the temporary setback. This mentality keeps him in the race long term. Being a legacy achiever is all about the long term.

Trait #6: Focus on Character

Focus more on your character than on your reputation.

—— John Wooden

Character is who you really are as a person while reputation is merely what others think of you.

Influential people feel good about how they present themselves to others, because they know they present the real person.

Sometimes the simple advice is the most important advice. I can remember being told in my youth that if I always told the truth I'd never have to worry about remembering what I said.

At the time I did not realize it, but I was being taught about integrity and character.

Legacy achievers wouldn't' have it any other way. Projecting an image that is inconsistent with who you really are is very dangerous. Many politicians have become painfully aware of this. When politicians win an election on false pretences they run the risk of being found out. Not only is the potential embarrassment great for these people, but the lack of credibility that stems from such a practice can be devastating. When a person's character is under attack they lose their influence.

To further emphasize this concept think of yourself as having a similar make up to the planet earth.

When we take a close look at ourselves we see a core, a mantel, and a surface-very much the same as our planet earth.

Our *core* is what we *really* believe as a person or who we really are. Our *mantel*, is our past experiences in life (something we can not change). And our *surface*, is how we appear to others.

It is easy to assume that a person is the "real deal" because they look good on the outside. But if we dig a little deeper, below the surface, we may find someone with core beliefs that don't match the surface. That person may have a mantle of experiences that we never would have imagined.

We can not change the past. Our mantle or life experiences may be filled with events that are not consistent with our current beliefs. It is more important that our core matches our surface than our surface matches our mantle.

Because we all make mistakes, our integrity and character should not be measured only by what we have done in the past. More importantly, it should be measured by how well our *current* actions match our *current* core values and beliefs.

If we tried to measure integrity and character by past experiences alone we would have no hope of becoming a better person. The one catch here is that when we have behaved in a way that is inconsistent with our current core beliefs it may take time for others to trust that we are truly different inside and out. That is why legacy achievers pay close attention to make sure that who they are is reflected by how they act.

Trait #7: Cultivate Courage

Influential people are courageous. In chapter 2, I explained that being in balance is about participating in activities rather than just avoiding them. It takes courage to face many of the challenges encountered each day. It also takes courage to admit our mistakes to ourselves and to others.

The opposite of courage is fear. Some people argue that fear provides a valuable service in preserving life by causing us to avoid danger. However, a closer look at fear reveals that other emotions act to preserve us from danger. Fear simply provides an alarm. When faced with danger, fear is an immediate response, but it paralyzes us if we don't convert our fear into a positive action emotion. Therefore fear triggers other emotions such as courage to guide us to safety.

Courage consists of two parts. The first part is focus. The more you focus on what you must do, the less weakening emotions such as fear will inhibit you.

When a wide receiver focuses clearly on the ball being thrown to him, he increases his chances of catching it. On the other hand, if he fears being tackled or dropping the ball, he tremendously reduces his odds for success. Focusing on the job at hand keeps negative emotions at bay. But to eliminate them we must add the second part of courage.

The second part of courage is enthusiasm. If the football player is focused but not enthusiastic, he leaves room for fear to creep in. Enthusiasm energizes focus and allows us to get the results we desire.

Legacy achievers often do not recognize themselves as being courageous because they plan for the future. When a person prepares for a challenge they are about to face, they enter the situation with assurance and do not need to be bolstered by courage.

A champion high diver who prepares for a difficult dive does not think about courage when taking the platform. Rather, the diver thinks about the technique. Preparation puts the diver's mind on a level where neither fear nor courage register. On this high performance level, the mind simply focuses enthusiastically on the task at hand.

~ ~ ~

 Motivation = B +  + C + H - RSE

 INFLUENCE

"If everyone is thinking alike then someone isn't thinking."

—— George S. Patton, Jr.

Chapter 4
The Tactical Dynamic Duo–
Creativity and Humor

Creativity

Creativity, an important tactical tool for developing motivation, has a rare quality. The more of it you use, the more you have at your command. Creativity is far more than a renewable resource; it's a fast-breeding reactor churning out more of itself every time it's turned on. Turn it on more often.

Legacy achievers show us that motivation is triggered during challenging times by thinking of a solution to our problems. Unmotivated people often feel there are no solutions for the challenges they face. This feeling stems from a hope-destroying lack of creativity. The simple act of deciding to use creativity to cope with our immediate situation will give us hope, and hope will motivate us to find the workable solutions we need.

At such times we say, "Why didn't I think of that?" or worse "Why'd I think of that and not act on it?"

If we trap ourselves into feeling there's no way out of a problem, we shut down. We think, "There's no reason to try. There's just no solution, why bother?"

Occasionally, in the midst of what appears to be a hopeless situation, we hear a story about an amazing person who rose above a similar situation, and we take heart. The solution conceived of renews our own motivation.

Tapping into our own creativity helps us maneuver around obstacles that block our motivation. Creative thinking creates successful solutions. In order to increase our creative skills, we must first recognize five common stumbling blocks to creativity.

Five Stumbling Blocks to Creativity

1. **"Somebody has already thought of it."**

When we rest on our laurels, and sit on our creativity, believing we've already thought of everything, it's only a matter of time before we're proven wrong. At such times we say, "Why didn't I think of that?" or worse "Why'd I think of that and not act on it?"

Consider an idea for a new product. Have you ever thought of a product that would solve an everyday consumer problem but say to yourself "Ah, someone probably invented it by now"? Then two years later you read an article about America's latest millionaire, only to find out that her ticket to fame and fortune was your idea. After trying to figure out

how she "stole your idea" logic sets in and you realize that she probably had the same idea but was wise enough to bring it to fruition.

2. "It's good enough."

An "It's good enough" attitude stifles creativity and stops motivation. The one-sided sliding-door minivan is a fine illustration of *good enough* thinking. Back in the 80s, this new adaptation of the older, larger vans was a very creative idea. But the only problem was that this new family vehicle, designed for convenience, had one of the most inconvenient features available, a sliding door on only one side.

Obviously the world loved the idea of a minivan because many where sold. But when the concept was developed further and two-sliding-door vans became available, sales of the improved models skyrocketed.

The car manufacturers who had an *it's-good-enough* attitude were caught behind the eight ball. Before they could redesign and retool, their competitors had skimmed the cream off the demand for the new double-door minivan.

3. "I'm not creative. I'm more analytical."

If we lock our minds into thinking, "I'm not creative. I'm analytical," we must reconsider. Analysis requires creativity. Creativity is the process that allows us to analyze effectively. So if one is creative-one is analytical.

Unfortunately, many people take themselves out of the creativity game before the buzzer sounds. I can assure you, we all have creativity. Our creativity acts like a muscle, the more we exercise it, the stronger it gets.

4. "What if I make a fool out of myself?"

Creativity requires some level of risk and risk creates fear. The fear of failure is a top creativity roadblock. We sometimes ask ourselves, "But what if I make a fool of myself? or "What if I make a mistake?" Thomas Edison is the greatest example I know of for overcoming this potential fear.

The story goes that Edison failed to invent the light bulb 9,999 times. But on try 10,000, he succeeded. When asked about the failures, Edison said he didn't fail even once. "I discovered 9,999 different ways light bulbs won't work." What an attitude!

If we fail, even a few times, we may feel like giving up. Instead, we should recall the motivational perspective that pushed Edison to creative success: In his mind, Edison made 10,000 discoveries!

5. "I don't have time for this."

Creative thinking can be time consuming. Tapping into creativity is an exercise in patience, if solutions to your problems don't readily appear overnight. Often, we must contemplate, process, and reprocess information to find imaginative answers. Like Edison we must contemplate, process, and repeat—until the light goes on.

We all Possess Creativity

Some people spend little time on original thinking, fully convinced of their lack of creativity. These people are quite convincing in their argument defending their lack of creative skills. But creativity is the only explanation for their powerful arguments, which defeats their point.

We all possess creativity. Children play creatively throughout the day as their attention wanders from toy to toy. Even without toys, kids find creative ways to play.

While all of my children are creative, my daughter Nicole provides our family with the most visual examples of her creativity. At the age of five she colors, decorates and redesigns anything she can get her hands on.

Unfortunately, sometimes her younger brother Ethan is the only malleable object she can get her hands on. She dresses him up in ways that crack up the entire family. Since he's too young to understand what she's doing to him, I usually rescue him out of good conscience. But sometimes I seize the opportunity to take a few pictures that will make his sixteenth birthday a lot more fun.

But as we rush into adulthood, we are often stripped of our creativity. In Daniel Burrus's book *Technotrends* (page 203, Harper Business) he references studies showing children losing as much as 90% of their creativity between the ages of five and seven. At around five, children enter formal educational systems and must conform to a more standardized way of thinking.

Conformity can suppress creativity. Although I'm a big believer in the benefits of conformity enhancing order in society, certain forms of conformity can flatten creativity. When we lose the ability to think creatively, we all suffer. As a result there are fewer new light bulbs to make our future a brighter place.

An excellent way to unlock creativity is to allow your mind to brainstorm combinations of two previously separate concepts—such as lightning and power, or two sliding doors and a minivan. You may find this exercise surprisingly rewarding and often very amusing.

We all posses the power to be creative, as psychologists who study creativity extensively all agree. I urge you to tap into your own creative capabilities.

Humor

A sense of humor is the component in the formula for motivation that can be a breath of fresh air when we need it most. There are three important benefits of humor which help legacy achievers increase and maintain motivation.

~ Better health
~ Greater understanding of other people's mistakes and enhanced power to forgive for our own missteps.
~ Increased ability to influence others

Better Health

Lee Berk, DrPH, MPH, and Stanley Tan, an Endocrinologist at California's Loma Linda University Medical Center, have been studying the effects of laughter on health. Since stress weakens the immune system, these doctors set out to determine whether and to what extent laughter strengthens the immune system.

Berk and Tan took blood samples from subjects in 10-minute intervals before, during, and after the subjects watched videos of comedians. They also did the same to a control group out of earshot of the TV.

The results where inspiring. Humor triggers similar physiological processes to exercise. The group who watched the comedians showed an increase in good hormones (endorphins and neurotransmitters) as well as two other hormones known to decrease levels of stress (cortisol and adrenaline). This occurs because laughter increases the number of cells producing antibodies such as T-cells which combat viruses.

Their research delivered a clear message: laughing more means you'll spend less time in the sick bed, and if you do get sick, you'll be back on your feet sooner. Now that's motivating!

On average, children laugh 150 times per day. Adults on the other hand, laugh only 10 times a day. When adults watch children play we often say, "Where do they get all that energy?" I believe children's ready laughter is the source of much of their energy. How much more energy would we adults have if we laughed as much as children?

Greater Understanding of Other People's Mistakes and Enhanced Power to Forgive Our Own Missteps

This greater capacity to understand and forgive mistakes can be illustrated through common occurrences. All of us at one time or another are frustrated by people whom we claim "just don't get it"

For example, take people who drive slowly in the fast lane. Have you ever noticed these people only do this with a car next to them so you can't pass! This drives most people crazy. When it happens to you, frustration turns to anger and anger turns to irrational conclusions. You think, "It's a conspiracy against me! That idiot must have gotten on the phone last night and called a few slow-driving friends just to tick me off!"

Now totally irrationally, you imagine the conversation, "Hey, Joe. What are you doing at 7:00 a.m.? See, I really want to bug this guy in a blue sedan. I'll get in front of his car and you box him in on the left, that way he can't pass. He'll go crazy. While we're at it, do you know anyone who's good at tailgating?"

Still boxed in, you conjure up countless new laws to stop the stupidity next to you, in front of you, now, even behind.

"Fine them $1,000 for each minute I'm late for work. No. Put people like that in jail for life. No. No. Put people like that in solitary confinement so they don't make the other inmates late, too. No one should have to suffer like this!"

Then, for some unknown reason, the slow driver hogging the fast lane moves to the slow lane, allowing you to pass. You can't wait to get a good look at the guy.

You creep right up next to him only to find it appears he just wasn't paying attention. He *just doesn't get it.* He wasn't even aware of your existence let alone your anger. You say to yourself: "What a fool!"

Then, one day you find yourself daydreaming in the fast lane. "Oops! I sure hope no one's behind me."

But of course, someone in a hurry is tailgating you. Embarrassed, you move to the slow lane, pretending to adjust your radio so that when the guy passes he won't think *you just didn't get it!*

It's a good time to laugh at yourself.

When we laugh at ourselves we learn to accept other people's mistakes with greater understanding. Laughing at our own mistakes is sometimes the only choice we have, outside of crying.

Years ago, as a guest on a Chicago radio show, I told the host I was searching for stories about people who *just don't get it.* The phone lines lit up. Furious people vented about others who *just don't get it.* Some complained about people who stand in line at fast food places for a long time, but when they finally reach the counter, they can't decide what to order. Others complained about people who stand still at the top of an escalator when they reach the top so other passengers have no place to exit. You name it, they complained about it!

One story came from a man who asked his girlfriend to buy a newspaper from a corner vending machine. He gave

her 50 cents and away she went, but she soon returned empty-handed.

"Where's my paper?"

"The machine was empty."

"Where's my 50 cents?"

"I don't have it anymore."

"Why not?"

"I didn't know the machine was empty until I dropped the quarters in the slot and opened the door because the newspaper in the window was in the way."

Now put yourself in his place. If your reaction to her dull insight is frustration then you rob yourself of a chance for laughter and create irritation, which steals your energy. If you really think about it, chances are you'll remember one or two "vending machine experiences" of your own.

I ran across a silly story in a book entitled, *The Best Book of Lists Ever*. While warming up for the New York Golden Gloves Championship in 1992, a boxer named Daniel Caruso punched himself so hard he couldn't compete.

You may think to yourself, "How stupid could you be? Punch yourself?" But if you're name is Dave Durand you'd say "Funny, but I can relate."

In my own kitchen one time, I showed a friend the difference between Tai fighting and kick-boxing. In a simple demonstration of how Tai fighters strike with their elbows, I accidentally punched myself in the nose and broke it. Whack! Crack!

There I stood with an amazed look on my face. My look of disbelief was only outdone by my friend's expression.

I pushed my nose back in place right then and there.

"Is it straight?" I asked, like I was fixing my tie.

"No," my friend said. "A little to the right. There you go."

I pushed my nose back in place right then and there. "Is it straight?" I asked, like I was fixing my tie. "No," my friend said. "A little to the right. There you go."

Oh yes, I felt pain, but I laughed at my odd situation. I never met Caruso, the boxer, but I sure can relate to his story.

Increased Ability to Influence Others.

Chapter Three discussed how being influential has a motivating effect on our lives. A good sense of humor can be an effective and inspiring part of influence. When we make people laugh, at ourselves or other things, we make others feel good. The physical benefits mentioned earlier affect our listeners. People pay psychiatrists thousands of dollars to help them feel better, but one good laugh can make a person feel better than six months of therapy—and it won't cost a dime.

We all have a tendency to like people who makes us laugh, and people who we like have the greatest edge when it comes to influencing us.

Creativity and Humor Together

Creativity plays a big role in our sense of humor. Laughter generates creativity. Creativity creates laughter. It's not everybody's aim in life to be a comedian, but we can all learn from the creative perspective a comedian has on many issues.

Comedians can take a totally normal life situation and, through creativity, twist it into a crazy scenario. The resulting laughter motivates the comedian to be even more creative. In turn, you enjoy more humor.

When comedian and talk show host Johnny Carson ended his last Tonight Show, people cried. When Seinfeld closed his series, fans across the country suffered from what they called "Seinfeld withdrawal." Why? Because, in a way, we lost people who made us laugh daily.

Laughter is one of the greatest gifts you can give another. We often feel grateful to people who make us laugh. In turn, we should spread a little laughter ourselves.

As I said, life's just too strange not to find the humor in it. Engage in humor. Combine your creativity with your sense of humor. After all, laughter helps us move past pain, and humor inspires the creativity from which motivation springs.

~ ~ ~

Chapter 5

Conclusion

You will benefit by the lessons we have learned from legacy achievers. Applying the formula for motivation enhances life tremendously. I will summarize the key points in the formula for motivation and then conclude with two stories I hope will add to your perspective on motivation.

Balance

Balancing our lives by spinning the six plates of life—family, finances, health, social contributions, education/vocation, and faith—is essential. Each of these balance points has the power to enhance our drive and appreciation for life; each of them also has the power to destroy. Having a daily focus on each one of the six is the main strategic key to unlocking perpetual motivation.

We need to be focused on a perfect target. We will never reach perfection, but using it as a target brings clarity to our goals. If we simply focus on doing our best, how will we know if we have arrived? How will we know if we couldn't continue to improve? The answer is difficult because being our best is hard to define. So stay focused on the endless target of perfection, but just like the pilot and copilot consider the times when you're a little off course to be part of your journey toward life's perfect balance.

Integrity Based Influence

We need to communicate with others in order to find balance in our lives and to become motivated by what we stand for. If we rely simply on the techniques taught by today's pop-culture trainers, we will only be effective for the short run.

The damage done to our reputation as well as our conscience can be difficult—or almost impossible—to repair. Because of this we must use integrity-based influence. That is, we must keep the good of the party we are influencing in mind. We must develop the seven IBI characteristics of legacy achievers.

1. Keep our emotions on a leash
2. Develop harmony and conviction in verbal communication
3. Anticipate (communication challenges and opportunities)
4. Be consistent
5. Develop a healthy outlook on competition
6. Focus on character
7. Be courageous

Creativity and Humor

Developing our creativity lets us get unstuck. We can feel trapped in life when we can't think of viable solutions to the problems we face. Creativity is the answer to such problems.

Our sense of humor can be essential in moving past difficult times, staying healthy, and allowing us to better understand other people. When we find humor in life, we can put our worries aside long enough to develop creative solutions. The result leads to our perpetual motivation.

Run away Self-Esteem

Possibly the most mind-bending insight acquired by reading this book is the different perspective on self-esteem. *Having* a high self-esteem is not the problem. Problems with self-esteem arise from how we attain it and whether we should focus on it.

A high self-esteem is the result of positive actions that need to be measured by outside standards in addition to our own. If we rely only on our standards—as many authors and psychiatrists recommend—we will be confused and overwhelmed by the ambiguity this brings. Likewise, if we try to build a false self-esteem through positive affirmations, which really constitute nothing more than lying to ourselves, we will never truly attain it.

We must submit to the preset standards of people and systems we respect, for example our family, corporation, or church. This will provide practical reasons to feel good about ourselves.

Let me emphasize the most important point in the chapter on runaway self-esteem: If we focus on serving others before we serve ourselves, we will become happy with who we are. We will be motivated to continue striving for the important things in life.

...we never actually live in the future. We only live in the present.

A Double Dose of Perspective

The following stories have morals that will add perspective on motivation. They will help you as you begin living a life filled with perpetual motivation.

If we live by the principles that we have been taught by legacy achievers, we are bound to find happiness. Unfortunately this thought may get us looking forward to the future so much that we forget to enjoy today. But when you really think about it, we never actually live in the future. We only live in the present.

John's story

Johnny was anxious to be big. He knew life would be better when he could see over the counter tops. When the great day arrived and he realized his goal, he knew he was almost old enough to go to kindergarten, where the fun would begin.

After the first week of kindergarten, Johnny could not stop thinking about what the first graders where doing in their classroom. He couldn't wait until he was in a real grade. After he arrived in first grade he repeated the same pattern of fantasizing about the following year, year after year. By the time Johnny was in eighth grade he knew he was only one year away from the ultimate life experience, high school. He wished each day away until high school finally arrived.

Johnny saw the upperclassmen and knew that they had it made. His desire to be the king of the school as a senior was great. That's when life would really begin. During Johnny's senior year he began to look into colleges. The thought of complete independence captured his attention. Every day of his senior year was spent longing for the freedom of college.

When John finally went off to university he began learning about science. He couldn't wait to some day be the head of a research company. He studied hard so he could finish his education as fast as possible. He graduated with honors and found a job.

He hated being at the bottom of the ladder. His boss seemed to have it made. Jonathon couldn't wait to have people reporting to him. In a few years he was promoted. He knew he was close to having it all. He just needed to buy the new car he had his eye on. Then he would have it made.

He bought the car but felt something was missing. He thought, "If I can climb the ladder at work I will be able to buy a house." Owning a home would be the answer to what is missing. So Jonathon worked hard and received the promotion. He was able to buy the house. But the house felt empty. Jonathon realized that his happiness would finally arrive when he was married.

Being attractive and having a dynamic personality made it easy for Jonathon to meet people. After a brief time dating, Jonathon met Miss Right and they married. But he thought there had to more. Having children would be the most fulfilling thing life could offer. So they had two children. But the work of taking care of infants and toddlers was more than Jonathon expected.

> Most legacy achievers would not categorize themselves as such.

When his children were out of diapers and able to talk, being a dad would be fulfilling, he knew. When his kids were able to walk and talk Jonathon realized they were only a few years away from being able to play catch. He knew it would be the time when they would bond. As the children grew and Jonathon turned into a taxi driver for them and their friends, he became anxious for the day when his kids could drive. As the kids acted as teenagers act, Jonathon exclaimed to himself that he could see the light at the end of the tunnel when the kids would go off to college and he would have the house back to the way it was before he had children.

That's when it hit him.

For the first time Jonathon realized he wanted something he already had. He had never stopped to enjoy today, the realization hitting him hard. What he was experiencing today is what he had looked forward to yesterday. Failing to understand this reality had kept him from living his life. With more than half of his life over, Jonathon had just started to live. It was time for him to meet the people in his life today, to live his life today, and to forget about hankering after tomorrow until it becomes today.

Each day is filled with treasures we need to discover and enjoy. Challenges sometimes make those treasures hard to find, but when we put our faith in God and focus on the people around us rather than on ourselves we can find fulfillment in our difficulties.

Hopefully you are able to gather some insight from the formula for living a motivated life, and from the legacy achievers who practice these principles. It is interesting to note that most legacy achievers would not categorize themselves as such. In a recent conversation I had with one of them who read this book, he said "Wow, I felt like you were writing about me when you wrote about people falling short of being legacy achievers."

I was surprised by his comment. I know him well and he has all of the traits and habits of a legacy achiever. He is a dedicated father and husband who prioritizes his family ahead of his job. He has reached business objectives and goals most people only dream about. He is responsible with his finances. He is a spiritual man focused on an increased faith, and he maintains great health. He is always motivated and a very happy person. That's the point. Although he does not see himself as a legacy achiever, he is one. He is in the constant growth mode and finds happiness in the process. He is excited about continuing to grow and is comfortable with his commitment to this lifelong journey. However, because he is focused on bettering himself, he feels he is not yet a legacy achiever.

We can always improve, no matter who we are. If we stop growing, we will die emotionally and physically. At the same time, we need to find happiness in the journey. If we wait for ourselves to arrive at a state of perfection while we are on earth in order to attain happiness, we will never find it.

The Long Day

The morning was so crisp it felt surreal. I knew it was going to be a great day. Although my travels have taken me to many places, I had never witnessed the scenic beauty I took in that day in the Rocky Mountains of British Columbia. The landscape was new to my eyes because I had arrived from Vancouver, after dark, the evening before in a rented Ford Explorer.

I would be finished with my meeting fairly early and be able to enjoy the breathtaking seven-hour drive back to Vancouver, this time in daylight. From there I would cruise the Pacific Coast by ferry boat for an hour before arriving on Vancouver Island and settling into my hotel, where I expected to enjoy a tasty meal and catch up on some reading. I would then get to sleep at a reasonable hour. At least that was my plan.

By late morning I was on my way, knowing I would be seeing the most incredible landscape in the world. The drive leaving Kelowna was filled with eye candy beyond visual taste bud capacity.

The jagged mountains in the distance melted into the closer rolling mountains sloping into Lake Okanagan. The lake is famous for Ogopogo, as its version of the Loch Ness monster is called. This sixty-mile-long, 900 foot deep, body of water draws the mind beyond its idyllic beauty into the mystery of the legend. Even people who consider themselves too sophisticated to believe in a lake monster seem to glance at the water in hopes of catching a glimpse of what they claim not to believe in.

As I drove out of the city and entered the heights of the massive Canadian Rockies, the world changed. My radio did not come in and my cell phone was out of range. I was alone in the midst of the beauty of God's creation, overwhelmed by the views surrounding me.

The seasons seemed to change from summer to spring as I went higher and higher. A snowstorm at the peak of the drive made it feel like winter. I couldn't wait to complete my trip to Vancouver Island, which is known for having some of the most beautiful gardens in the world. I was right; today was a great day.

Making good time, I entered the City of Vancouver as planned, six hours after starting. Unfortunately, the rush hour had just begun.

Vancouver's beauty is as impressive as its road system is not. Many travelers get to enjoy the landscape from their car windows longer than they would prefer. I was about to have the experience of enjoying the view for an hour longer than expected. Mentally I could handle it until I made a huge mistake.

To save time I decided to rely on directional signs to get me to the ferry instead of stopping for directions. This soon put me in the middle of downtown Vancouver stuck in a lane of traffic that, before I could not get out of, forced me onto the Lion Gate Bridge. A sign seemed to say it was the right way to go.

Wrong.

My penalty was an hour and a half ride across a bridge spanning less than a half mile, plus an additional hour and half to get back. All of a sudden my seven-hour car ride had turned into at least ten, probably eleven, hours. Now time pressed.

I asked for directions, and things seemed like they were about to get better.

Wrong again.

My friendly direction givers spoke with too much conviction to be doubted when they told me how to find the ferry ten minutes away. But somehow I was misled. I traveled everywhere a ten-minute drive would cover. No ferry.

My blood felt searing hot under my skin. My anger clouded my mind so much I was driving recklessly. I even ran a red light because I wasn't paying attention, avoiding a side-on collision by about a half second. I hate to imagine how the lives of all those involved in the near-accident would have changed had either car been moving at a slightly different speed.

I could hardly calm down. When I did, I went to a gas station where two young gentlemen looked like they might be able to help me. I will never forget telling them to talk to me like I was two bricks short of a load.

"Guys, keep the directions simple because I must be lacking the mental capacity to follow basic instructions today. Everyone tells me the ferry is ten minutes away and I have been everywhere within ten minutes from here. Speak slowly and draw me pictures because I am at my wits' end!"

They laughed and said "Ten minutes, no way. The ferry is at least an hour from here."

I couldn't believe it—a whole hour away! At this point I had forgotten about getting to the hotel in time for a nice dinner, I just wanted to get to the ferry before it sailed at 11:00 p.m. I had to catch the last boat to the island or miss my meeting the following morning. It was already after 10:00 so I had to move fast.

He looked amazed and said, "The fire." "The fire?" I asked.

Because I was irrationally suspicious of everyone's ability to provide sound directions, I crossed the street to see if I could get corroboration. To my delight I received confirming directions. Out of curiosity I asked:

"How long will it take to get there?"

"About ten minutes."

I almost fell over. How could that be? I didn't waste time worrying about it and arrived barely soon enough to drive aboard the night's last boat. I parked my car on the ferry's lower parking level along with what looked like several hundred cars.

Feeling nauseous from hunger, headache, and bad attitude, I struggled to climb to the cafeteria-style restaurant on the ferry's top floor—four decks up if I remember correctly. I wanted to eat something and then rest until we reached the island.

At the counter I selected my food and went to a quiet corner to relax. Right away a hairy lumberjack-looking fellow, who apparently needed to talk to someone, sat down next to me. I was not in the mood for conversation.

"So where are you headed?"

I thought his question was a bit silly since the ferry had only one destination—the island—but something about him made me want to be polite.

"Victoria."

"Where in Victoria?"

"I don't know yet. I'll choose a hotel when I get there."

What he said next ended my coma-like state, and put me into a close cousin of the fight of flight mode, weakness forgotten.

"You're screwed. The whole island is sold out because of the jazz festival."

...everyone is great at being great when things are going great, but truly great people are great at being great when things aren't going so great.

I jumped up, ran four flights down to my car, got my cell phone, returned to a tourist brochure display on the top floor, and started calling hotels. Finally I found what I'm sure was the *last* hotel room on the entire island.

It was my first experience with a room honored by that description, and I soon found out why it had earned the distinction. The two-story hotel was smaller than a university frat house. It was after 1 a.m. when I got there, stumbling with exhaustion and not too clear-headed. After checking for roaches and rats, I tried to call my wife.

I always call Lisa when I arrive at a hotel, no matter how late. She always wants to know where I am and how I'm doing; I also want to know how she and the kids are doing. I couldn't get through on my cell phone and my calling card didn't work. I would have to talk to her the next day.

I slept like a rock. The next morning, feeling refreshed and eager to start the new day, I decided to say a kind word to the hotel owner before going on my way. As I walked down, I met him.

He looked at me with great concern and said, "I'm so sorry." I glanced over my shoulder to see who he was talking to, but saw no one.

"I'm so sorry," he said again.

"About what?"

He looked puzzled and then added a *so*, "I'm so, so sorry."

"About what?" I repeated, louder this time.

"The fire," he said, looking amazed.

"The fire? What fire?"

In the middle of the night the hotel had caught on fire and was evacuated, he told me. The street had been lined with fire engines and teeth-chattering hotel guests in pajamas.

I had slept through the whole thing and no one knew I was in the hotel while it was burning. My wife didn't know where I was, no one knew.

Then it hit me: I was being watched over and cared for. During the previous mistake and blunder-filled day I had never stopped to appreciate my greatest possession, the gift of life. Even narrowly escaping death while running the red light did not get me to appreciate life the way I did that morning.

My attitude became one of gratitude. It had been eight years since I began studying motivation and life balance, but it took only one twenty-four-hour period to convince me that a simple appreciation for my gift of life is a powerful motivation for living the best life I am capable of living.

Although not a formal part of the formula for motivation, the concept of appreciating life resides in the hearts of legacy achievers. Take an inventory of what God has given you. When we have a true appreciation for life, it will be reflected by our love for others, our peace during challenging times, and our ability to stay motivated.

... the concept of appreciating life resides in the hearts of legacy achievers.

Along the road, there will be challenges. Here's a helpful thought to carry with you: everyone is great at being great when things are going great, but truly great people are great at being great when things aren't going so great. When faced with challenges, look at the ways your life will improve when you gain the experience and skills it will take to overcome them.

We don't need to become famous, rich, or popular to become a legacy achiever. All we need to do is to stay loyal to the things that are most important in life. Through this focus, we will find motivation and make an impact that will be remembered as a legacy.

God Bless!

More Inspiring

Products . . .

This Book & Other Products

For information on bulk purchases of **Perpetual Motivation** or to inquire about any other ProBalance products including Dave Durand's **Perpetual Motivation Planner, the "Balander™"** contact us at the address or phone number provided below.

Balander™ by Durand

(The Perpetual Motivation Time Management System)

Available in leather and vinyl; Regal edition (full size); Compact edition; Purse edition.

This daily planner is the most efficient planner available today. The patented layout has a series of die cuts and perforations that allow you to see your day, week, month and year all at once, while still providing plenty of note taking and planning room. The Balander™ is designed to keep you motivated with highlighted areas for each of the six balance points.

Video tapes

~ "Financial Management for Young Adults" recommended for ages 15-23

~ "Kickin abs" Dave Durand's original karate aerobic video

Audio Tapes

~ *"The Pursuit of Life's Perfect Balance"* by Dave Durand
4 hours of detailed balance training on the 6 balance points.

Speaking Engagements

To inquire about these products or to book Dave Durand for a speaking engagement please contact:

~ Order Today ~

ProBalance

~

888-474-3162

~

www.davedurand.com

~

ProBalance
P.O. box 298
Big Bend, WI 53103-0298

Notes